Lecture Notes in Computer Science 12834

More information about this subseries at http://www.springer.com/series/7407

Viktória Zsók · John Hughes (Eds.)

Trends in Functional Programming

22nd International Symposium, TFP 2021
Virtual Event, February 17–19, 2021
Revised Selected Papers

 Springer

Editors
Viktória Zsók 🆔
Eötvös Loránd University
Budapest, Hungary

John Hughes 🆔
Chalmers University of Technology
Göteborg, Sweden

ISSN 0302-9743   ISSN 1611-3349 (electronic)
Lecture Notes in Computer Science
ISBN 978-3-030-83977-2   ISBN 978-3-030-83978-9 (eBook)
https://doi.org/10.1007/978-3-030-83978-9

LNCS Sublibrary: SL1 – Theoretical Computer Science and General Issues

This Springer imprint is published by the registered company Springer Nature Switzerland AG
The registered company address is: Gewerbestrasse 11, 6330 Cham, Switzerland

Preface

This volume contains selected papers presented at the 22nd International Symposium on Trends in Functional Programming (TFP 2021), held online during February 17–19, 2021. The conference was collocated with 10th International Workshop on Trends in Functional Programming in Education (TFPIE 2021) and Lambda Days 2021.

TFP is an international forum for researchers with interests in all aspects of functional programming, taking a broad view of current and future trends in this area. It aspires to be a lively environment for presenting the latest research results and other contributions, with an unconventional reviewing process that allows for full single blind peer review either before or after the symposium (or both, if the pre-symposium reviews ask for changes that need a second review before inclusion in the proceedings).

Each paper received three reviews in each round. This year 18 papers were submitted in total (10 reviewed before the symposium and 8 afterwards), and 15 of them were presented, together with the keynote by Prof. Zhenjiang Hu (Peking University, China) on "Constructive Bidirectional Programming". After the final reviewing round, revised versions of 6 papers were selected for inclusion in this proceedings. The final selection spans across nested parallelism, semantics, task-oriented programming, modeling, translating, and proving functional programs.

TFP offers two prizes: the John McCarthy award for the best paper and the David Turner award for the best student paper. The paper "Dataset Sensitive Autotuning of Multi-versioned Code Based on Monotonic Properties: Autotuning in Futhark" by Philip Munksgaard, Svend Lund Breddam, Troels Henriksen, Fabian Cristian Gieseke, and Cosmin Oancea was awarded the best paper prize. The paper "A Generic Back-end for Exploratory Programming" by Damian Frolich and L. Thomas van Binsbergen was awarded the best student paper prize.

All of this was only possible thanks to the hard work of the authors and of the Program Committee members. We are deeply grateful to both.

The event was sponsored by Facebook for which we are grateful.

June 2021

Viktória Zsók
John Hughes

Organization

Program Committee Chairs

Viktória Zsók   Eötvös Loránd University, Budapest, Hungary
John Hughes   Chalmers University of Technology, Gothenburg, Sweden

Program Committee

Peter Achten   Radboud University, Nijmegen, The Netherlands
Jost Berthold   Digital Asset, Sydney, Australia
Stephen Chang   University of Massachusetts Boston, Bostan, USA
Olaf Chitil   University of Kent, Canterbury, UK
João Paulo Fernandes   University of Coimbra, Coimbra, Portugal
Jeremy Gibbons   University of Oxford, Oxford, UK
Andrew Gill   University of Kansas, Lawrence, USA
Clemens Grelck   University of Amsterdam, Amsterdam, The Netherlands
Jurriaan Hage   Utrecht University, Utrecht, The Netherlands
Pieter Koopman   Radboud University, Nijmegen, The Netherlands
Hans-Wolfgang Loidl   Heriot-Watt University, Edinburgh, UK
Marco T. Morazán   Seton Hall University, New Jersey, USA
João Saraiva   University of Minho, Braga, Portugal

Additional Reviewers

Jianhao Li
Ábel Sinkovics

Contents

Nested Parallelism, Semantics, Task-Oriented Programming

Dataset Sensitive Autotuning
of Multi-versioned Code Based
on Monotonic Properties
Autotuning in Futhark

Philip Munksgaard$^{(\boxtimes)}$ ⓘ, Svend Lund Breddam, Troels Henriksen ⓘ,
Fabian Cristian Gieseke ⓘ, and Cosmin Oancea ⓘ

DIKU, University of Copenhagen, Copenhagen, Denmark
philip@munksgaard.me, athas@sigkill.dk, fabian.gieseke@di.ku.dk,
cosmin.oancea@diku.dk

Abstract. Functional languages allow rewrite-rule systems that aggressively generate a multitude of semantically-equivalent but differently-optimized code versions. In the context of GPGPU execution, this paper addresses the important question of how to compose these code versions into a single program that (near-)optimally discriminates them across different datasets. Rather than aiming at a general autotuning framework reliant on stochastic search, we argue that in some cases, a more effective solution can be obtained by customizing the tuning strategy for the compiler transformation producing the code versions.

We present a simple and highly-composable strategy which requires that the (dynamic) program property used to discriminate between code versions conforms with a certain *monotonicity assumption*. Assuming the monotonicity assumption holds, our strategy guarantees that if an optimal solution exists it will be found. If an optimal solution doesn't exist, our strategy produces human tractable and deterministic results that provide insights into what went wrong and how it can be fixed.

We apply our tuning strategy to the incremental-flattening transformation supported by the publicly-available Futhark compiler and compare with a previous black-box tuning solution that uses the popular OpenTuner library. We demonstrate the feasibility of our solution on a set of standard datasets of real-world applications and public benchmark suites, such as Rodinia and FinPar. We show that our approach shortens the tuning time by a factor of 6× on average, and more importantly, in five out of eleven cases, it produces programs that are (as high as 10×) faster than the ones produced by the OpenTuner-based technique.

Keywords: Autotuning · GPGPU · Compilers · Nested parallelism · Flattening · Performance

This research has been partially supported by the Independent Research Fund Denmark grant under the research project *FUTHARK: Functional Technology for High-performance Architectures*.

V. Zsók and J. Hughes (Eds.): TFP 2021, LNCS 12834, pp. 3–23, 2021.
https://doi.org/10.1007/978-3-030-83978-9_1

1   Introduction

Adapting the compilation technique to the dataset and hardware characteristics is an important research direction [8], especially in the functional context where rewrite-rule systems can, in principle, be used to aggressively generate a multitude of semantically-equivalent but differently-optimized versions of code [27].

The main target of this work is highly-parallel hardware, such as GPGPUs, which have been successfully used to accelerate a number of big-compute/data applications from various fields. Such systems are however notoriously difficult to program when the application exhibits nested parallelism—think imperfectly-nested parallel loops whose sizes are statically unknown/unpredictable.

Common parallel-programming wisdom says that, in principle, one should exploit enough levels of parallelism to fully utilize the hardware[1] and to efficiently sequentialize the parallelism in excess. However, even this simple strategy is difficult to implement when the parallel sizes vary significantly across (classes of) datasets: for example, one dataset may offer enough parallelism in the top parallel loop, while others require exploiting several levels of inner parallelism.

To make matters even more difficult, the common wisdom does not always hold: in several important cases [3,14] it has been shown that even when the outer parallelism is large enough, exploiting inner levels of parallelism is more efficient, e.g., when the additional parallelism can be mapped to the threads of a Cuda block, and when the intermediate results fit in shared memory.[2] Finally, the best optimization strategy may not even be portable across different generations of the same type of hardware (GPU) from the same vendor [19].[3]

In essence, for many important applications, there is no silver-bullet optimization recipe producing one (statically-generated) code version resulting in optimal performance for all datasets and hardware of interest. A rich body of work has been aimed at solving this pervasive problem, for example by applying:

1. supervised offline training techniques to infer the best configuration of compiler flags that results in *best-average* performance across datasets [5,8,13];
2. various compile-time code-generation recipes for *stencil* applications, from which the best one is selected offline by stochastic methods and used online to compute same-shape stencils on larger arrays [12,15,24];
3. dynamic granularity-control analysis [2,28] aimed at multicore execution, but which require runtime-system extensions that are infeasible on GPUs.

Such solutions (1–2) however, do not aim to cluster classes of datasets to the code version best suited for them, and thus to construct a single program

---

[1] Current GPU hardware require about a hundred thousands of concurrent threads to reach peak performance, and the number is still growing according to Moore's law.

[2] In Cuda, shared memory refers to a small and fast memory that is used as a user-managed cache, and enables inter-thread communication within a block of threads.

[3] The LocVolCalib benchmark of FinPar suite [3], run on the **large** dataset, favors the common-wisdom approach on a Kepler GPU, but prefers exploiting inner levels of parallelism on a Turing GPU. Matters can only worsen across hardware vendors.

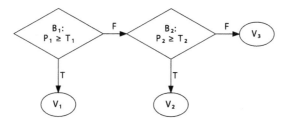

Fig. 1. The tuning tree of the paper's running examples. $V_{1...3}$ are code versions and $B_{1...2}$ are the predicates discriminating them. $P_{1...2}$ are the degree of parallelism exploited by $V_{1...2}$ and $T_{1...2}$ are the thresholds subject to autotuning.

that offers optimal performance for all datasets. Instead, a promising technique, dubbed *incremental flattening* [19], has been studied in the context of Futhark language [11,18]: semantically-equivalent code versions are statically generated—by incrementally mapping increasing levels of application parallelism to hardware parallelism—and are combined into one program by guarding each of them with a predicate that compares the amount of exploited parallelism of that version with a externally defined threshold variable (integer), see Fig. 1.

The amount of exploited parallelism is a dynamic program property (known at runtime), while the threshold values are found by offline tuning on a set of representative datasets. The proposed autotuner [19] uses a black-box approach that relies heavily on the stochastic heuristics of OpenTuner [4], but is impractical for application development and mainstream use, as demonstrated in Sect. 4 on a number of standard datasets of real-world applications [14,16] and public benchmarks from Rodinia [7] and FinPar [3] suites:

- even relatively "simple" programs, i.e., exhibiting a small number of thresholds, may result in unpredictable and suboptimal tuning times;
- the approach does not scale well, because the search space grows exponentially with the number of thresholds,[4] and thus an optimal result that perfectly discriminates between code versions may not be found, even if it exists.

1.1 Scope and Contributions of This Paper

Instead of aiming to implement a general flavor of autotuning (e.g., relying on stochastic search), this paper argues in favor of promoting a tighter compiler-autotuner codesign, by customizing the tuning technique to the code transformation producing the multi-versioned code. Our framework assumes that the multi-versioned program has the structure of a forest[5] of tuning trees, such as the one depicted in Fig. 1, namely that code versions $V_{1...3}$ are placed inside branches $B_{1...2}$, whose conditions compare a dynamic program property (value) $P_{1...2}$

---

[4] A program may consist of several computational kernels, and each such kernel may produce multi-versioned code, hence the number of thresholds can grow large.

[5] Each tuning tree corresponds to a computational kernel of the original program.

against *one* freshly introduced unknown/threshold variable $T_{1...2}$. Our framework finds an optimal integral value for each threshold as long as the dynamic properties (P_i) conform with a *monotonic assumption*, namely:

If for a certain dynamic program value P_i, the corresponding code version V_i is found to be faster/slower than any/a combination of versions belonging to the subtree at the right of B_i, then it will remain faster/slower for any dynamic program value greater/less than P_i.

If the dynamic program value refers to the utilized parallelism, the trivial intuition for monotonicity is that if a code version parallelizes only the outermost loop, and has been found optimal for some loop count, then increasing the count of that parallel loop should not require exploiting the parallelism of inner loops. One can similarly reason for (combined) properties referring to load balancing, thread divergence, or locality of reference. Conversely, our technique is not suitable for tuning tile sizes, for example.

These limitations enable the design of a simple, but highly-composable and practically-effective tuning strategy. We present the intuition by using the tuning tree of Fig. 1 and the simplifying assumption that the dynamic property values P_i do not change during the execution of a dataset. Then autotuning should select (exactly) one code version per (training) dataset. The rationale is as follows:

For a fixed dataset d, we can always find an instantiation of threshold values that exercises V_3 and then V_2, and we can measure their runtime. We can now combine V_2 and V_3 into an optimal subprogram on d, named V_2', by assigning T_2 *the maximal interval* that selects the fastest of the two, i.e., $[0, P_2]$ if V_2 is faster and $[P_2 + 1, \infty]$ otherwise—please notice that maximizing the interval is sound under the monotonic assumption. We continue in a recursive fashion to compute the interval of T_1 that discriminates between V_1 and subprogram V_2'.

Once we have (independently) computed partial solutions for each training dataset, we compute a global solution for each threshold by intersecting the maximal intervals across datasets. It is easy to see, by definition of intersection and maximal intervals, that (i) the resulted intervals are maximal, (ii) if nonempty, then any instantiation of the resulting intervals optimally satisfies each dataset, and (iii) conversely, if empty, then no solution exists that optimally satisfies all datasets—we use the term "near-optimal" to accommodate the empty case. Furthermore, this rationale naturally extends to the general case in which the values of P_i might vary during the execution of a dataset (see Sect. 3.5).

In this case, the maximal interval of T_i that perfectly discriminates versions V_i and V_{i+1} is found by binary searching the set of m_i distinct values taken by P_i. This requires $O(log_2 \ m_i)$ program runs, instead of $O(1)$ in the simple case.

In comparison with solutions reliant on stochastic search, our technique:

- processes each dataset independently and composably between code versions, thus requiring a predictable and small number of program runs;
- produces a guaranteed optimal solution that perfectly discriminates the training datasets if the resulting intervals are non-empty;[6]

---

[6] Of course, the accuracy of classifying new (test) datasets depends on whether the training datasets capture the sweet points—this is the user's responsibility.

– produces human tractable, deterministic[7] results, which, if sub-optimal, provide insight into what went wrong (empty intervals) and how it can be fixed. For example, one can consider only the maximal set of datasets that produces non-empty intervals, or one can possibly instruct the compiler to generate the code versions in a different order or even redundantly, see Sect. 3.4.

The information used by our autotuner requires minimal and trivial compiler modifications that add profiling printouts to the resulting code (details in Sect. 3.1), hence our framework can be easily ported to other compilers employing similar multi-versioned analysis.

We demonstrate the benefits of our approach by applying it to Futhark's incremental flattening analysis and evaluating a number of (i) real-world applications [14, 16] from the remote-sensing and financial domains and (ii) benchmarks from standard suites, such as Rodinia [7] and Finpar [3, 20]. In comparison with the OpenTuner-based implementation, our method reduces the tuning time by a factor as high as 22.6× and on average 6.4×, and in 5 out of the 11 cases it finds better thresholds that speed-up program execution by as high as 10×.

2 Background

This section provides a brief overview of the Cuda and Futhark features necessary to understand this paper.

2.1 Brief Overview of Cuda

Cuda [1] is a programming model for Nvidia GPGPUs. Writing a Cuda program requires the user to explicitly (de-)allocate space on the GPU device, and to copy the computation input and result between the host (CPU) and device (GPU) memory spaces. The GPU-executed code is written as a Cuda kernel and executed by all threads. The parallel iteration space is divided into a grid of blocks of threads, where the grid and block can have up to three dimensions. The threads in a block can be synchronized by means of barriers, and they can communicate by using a small amount of fast/scratchpad memory, called shared memory. The shared memory is intended as a user-managed cache, since it has much smaller latency—one-to-two orders of magnitude—than the global memory. The global memory is accessible to all threads, but in principle no synchronization is possible across threads in different blocks—other than terminating the kernel, which has full-barrier semantics.

2.2 Incremental Flattening

Futhark [11, 18] uses a conventional functional syntax. Futhark programs are written as a potentially-nested composition of second-order array combinators (SOACs) that have inherently-parallel semantics—such as map, reduce, scan,

---

[7] It produces the same result modulo variances in execution time.

```
1  let mapscan1 [m][n] (xss: [m][n]i32) : [m][n]i32 =
2      map2 (\(row: [n]i32) (i: i32) ->
3          loop (row: [n]i32) for _ in 0 ..< 64 do
4              let row' = map (+ i) row
5              in scan (+) 0 row'
6          )
7          xss (0 ..< m)
```

Fig. 2. Futhark program with size-invariant parallelism.

scatter, generalized histograms [17]—and loops that are always executed sequentially. Loops have the semantics of a tail recursive function, and they explicitly declare the variables that are variant throughout the execution of the loop.

Figure 2 shows the contrived but illustrative mapscan1 function that is used as a running example in this paper. The function takes as input a $m \times n$ matrix and produces a $m \times n$ matrix as result (line 1). The function body maps each row of the input matrix and each row number i with a lambda function (line 2) that consists of a loop that iterates 64 times (line 3). The loop-variant variable row is initialized with the row i of the xss matrix, and the result of the loop-body expression will provide the input for the next iteration. The loop body adds i to each element of row (line 4), and computes all prefix sums of the result (line 5).

One can observe that mapscan1 has two levels of imperfectly-nested parallelism: the outer map at line 2 and the inner map-scan composition at lines 4-5, but the Cuda model essentially supports only flat parallelism. The application parallelism is mapped to the hardware by the incremental-flattening analysis [19], which builds on Blelloch's transformation [6][8] but is applied incrementally:

V_1: a first code version is produced by utilizing only the parallelism of the outer map of size m, and sequentializing the inner map-scan composition.

V_2: a second code version (that uses $m \times n$ parallelism) is produced that maps the outer map parallelism on the Cuda grid, sets the Cuda block size to the size n of inner parallelism, and performs the inner map-scan composition in parallel by each Cuda block of threads. The intermediate arrays row and row' are maintained and reused from Cudas fast shared memory.

V_3: the flattening procedure is (recursively) applied, for example by interchanging the outer map inside the loop, and by distributing it across the inner map and scan expressions. The arrays will be maintained in global memory. In principle, if the nested-parallel depth is greater than 2, then the recursive application will produce many more code versions.

Unfortunately, when flattening mapscan1, we don't statically know what the different degrees of parallelism will be, because they depend on the input data. If the input matrix is very tall, we might prefer to use the outer parallelism and sequentialize the inner, and vice versa if the matrix is wide. Essentially, each

---

[8] Blelloch's flattening also work in the presence of divide-and-conquer recursion, but Futhark does not support recursive functions.

of the three generated code versions $V_{1..3}$ might be the best one for a class of datasets. As mentioned earlier, Futhark will generate all three code versions and arrange them in a tuning tree as shown in Fig. 1, where the dynamic program property refers to the degree of parallelism utilized by a certain code version, e.g., $P_1 = m$ and $P_2 = n$ (or $P_2 = m \cdot n$).

3   Autotuning Framework

3.1   Tuning Forests, Program Instrumentation

While the introduction has presented the intuition in terms of the tuning tree of Fig. 1, the structure used by the tuner is essentially a tuning forest, because:

1. a program may consist of multiple computational kernels, each of them potentially generating multi-version code, and
2. the recursive step of incremental flattening may split the original computation by means of (outer)-map fission into multiple kernels, each of them potentially generating multiple code versions.

Other than the high-level structure that discriminates between code versions—i.e., the branches $B_{1..2}$—the tuning-forest representation is completely oblivious to the control flow in which various code versions are (arbitrarily) nested in. The only manner in which this control flow is (indirectly) observable by and relevant to the tuning framework is by the fact that a dynamic property P_i may take multiple values during the execution of one dataset, e.g., if a code version is executed inside a loop then its degree of parallelism may also be loop variant. Our approach requires (minimal) compiler instrumentation, added to determine:

1. the structure of the tuning forest: this is static information documenting the control dependencies between thresholds: in Fig. 1, T_2 depends on T_1 because the code versions V_2 and V_3, are only executed when $P_1 \geq T_1$ fails.
2. dynamic information corresponding to the dynamic property (degree of parallelism) of each executed kernel instance, and the *overall* running time of the application. Importantly, we do not require the ability to perform fine-grained profiling of program fragments.

3.2   Autotuning Overview

The key insight of the tuning algorithm is that one can perform the tuning independently for each dataset, and that the result of tuning each threshold is a maximal interval. Furthermore, the threshold interval can be found by performing a bottom-up traversal of the tuning forest, where each step tunes one threshold (also individually). Finally, a globally-optimal solution can be found by intersecting the locally-optimal intervals across all datasets and then selecting any value in the resulting interval (as long as the training datasets are representative). This is sound and guarantees that a near-optimal solution will be

```
 1: function TUNEPROGRAM(p, ds)
 2:     ▷ p is the program being run
 3:     ▷ ds are the training datasets
 4:     ▷ t̄ = t₁, . . . , tₙ are p's thresholds in the order they appear in the tuning graph
 5:     r_{t_i} ← (0, ∞) for each program threshold t_i, 1 ≤ i ≤ n
 6:     for d in ds do
 7:         t_i ← ∞, ∀1 ≤ i ≤ n
 8:         bestRun ← run p on d with values (t₁, . . . , tₙ)
 9:         for i in n . . . 1 do
10:             ((lb_i, ub_i), bestRun) ← TUNETHRESHOLD(p, d, t̄, i, bestRun)
11:             t_i ← (lb_i + ub_i)/2
12:             r_{t_i} ← r_{t_i} ∩ (lb_i, ub_i)
13:         end for
14:     end for
15:     return (r_{t₁}, . . . , r_{tₙ})
16: end function
```

Fig. 3. Algorithm for tuning a program across a set of training datasets. For a given dataset, the near-optimal interval for each threshold is (individually) determined during a bottom-up traversal of the tuning tree (forest), where the previously determined thresholds values are used for subsequent runs. The partial results are aggregated across all datasets by taking the intersection of the corresponding intervals.

found (if one exists) as long as the dynamic program property used as driver for autotuning conforms with the following monotonic assumption:

If for a certain dynamic program value P_i, a code version V_i is found to be faster/slower than any/a combination of versions belonging to the subtree at the right of B_i, then it will remain faster/slower for any dynamic program value greater/less than P_i.

The driver of the tuning algorithm is implemented by the function TUNE-PROGRAM, presented in Fig. 3, which takes as arguments a program p and a set of training datasets ds and produces a globally-optimal interval r_{t_i} for each threshold $t_i, 1 \leq i \leq n$. The outer loop starting on line 6 iterates over the available datasets. For each dataset, all thresholds are first set to infinity (line 7), forcing the bottom-most code version to run, e.g. V_3 in Fig. 1. Running that code version and timing it (line 8) provides a baseline for further tuning. The loop on lines 9–13 tunes each threshold in bottom-up order. After finding the optimal threshold interval for each threshold (line 10), the threshold is set to an arbitrary value in the locally optimal interval (line 11) and finally the interval is intersected with the globally optimal interval found so far (line 12).

3.3 Tuning Size-Invariant Thresholds on a Single Dataset

When tuning a single threshold, we need to distinguish between *size-variant* and *size-invariant* branches. If during the execution of the given program on *a single dataset*, we call a particular branch B_i size-invariant if, whenever it is encountered in the tuning-graph, the corresponding dynamic program value,

```
1: function TUNETHRESHOLDINVAR(p, d, t̄, i, bestRun)
2:     ePar ← EXPLOITEDPAR(p, d, tᵢ)
3:     tᵢ ← 0
4:     newRun ← run p on d with threshold values t̄
5:     if new < best + ε then
6:         bestRun ← min(newRun, bestRun)
7:         lbᵢ ← 0, ubᵢ ← ePar
8:     else
9:         lbᵢ ← ePar + 1, ubᵢ ← ∞
10:    end if
11:    return ((lbᵢ, ubᵢ), bestRun)
12: end function
```

Fig. 4. Tuning algorithm for a size-invariant threshold. EXPLOITEDPAR(p, d, t) is the constant amount of parallelism of the code version guarded by threshold t on dataset d.

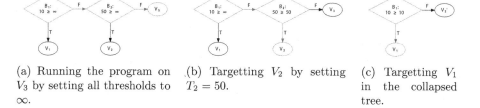

(a) Running the program on V_3 by setting all thresholds to ∞.

(b) Targetting V_2 by setting $T_2 = 50$.

(c) Targetting V_1 in the collapsed tree.

Fig. 5. Tuning the bottom-most threshold of the tuning-graph on a single dataset.

P_i, is constant. If P_i can change during a single execution, we call the branch size-variant. As an example, it is clearly the case that `mapscan1` of Fig. 2 is size-invariant, because the parallel sizes do not change during execution, hence neither does the degree of parallelism of each code version.

Because the degree of parallelism never changes, it stands to reason that for a given branch we should always perform the same choice: Either use the guarded code version or progress further down the tree. Therefore, in order to find the optimal threshold value for the given input, we have to time the guarded code version, compare it to the best run time found further down the tree, and pick a threshold value that chooses the fastest of the two.

Figure 4 shows the pseudocode of a version of TUNETHRESHOLD for tuning a single size-invariant threshold on a given dataset by doing exactly that. The arguments correspond to the arguments given to TUNETHRESHOLD in Fig. 3. The idea is simple: Whenever TUNETHRESHOLDINVAR is called on a threshold T_i, all the thresholds further down the tree (T_j where $j > i$) have already been tuned, and the best run time that has been encountered so far is `bestRun`. Therefore, we need to run the program once using the code version guarded by T_i (done on line 4 of Fig. 4) to determine if it is faster than any of the previously tested code versions. If it is, the optimal threshold interval for T_i is the one that always

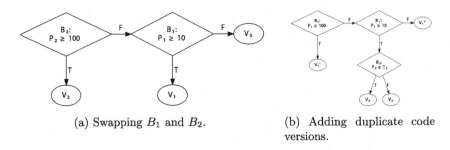

(a) Swapping B_1 and B_2.

(b) Adding duplicate code versions.

Fig. 6. Alternative versions of the tuning graph, enabling different constraints.

chooses V_i, namely the interval from 0 to P_i (lines 6–7). Otherwise the interval from $P_i + 1$ to ∞ is optimal (line 8). As stated in the introduction, taking the maximal interval is sound under the monotonic assumption.

Figure 5 shows an example of how the size-invariant tuning works. In Fig. 5a all thresholds are set to ∞, forcing V_3 to run. That allows us to find the baseline performance and get the dynamic program values $P_1 = 10$ and $P_2 = 50$. Then, in Fig. 5b, We use the knowledge of P_2 to force V_2 to run. The change in overall run time of the program represents the difference between running code versions V_3 and V_2. After choosing an optimal threshold, we can think of the bottom part of the tree as one collapsed node, and continue our tuning by moving up the tree to run V_1, as seen in figure Fig. 5c

3.4   Monotonicity Assumption

The monotonicity assumption, outlined in Sect. 1.1, is what ultimately makes our tuning method work, and it is therefore also the primary restriction for our method. In essence, we assume that for any branch B_i, the performance of the guarded code version as a function of P_i, is monotonically increasing compared with any of the code versions further down the tree. In terms of Fig. 5, if V_1 is found to outperform any of the other versions when $P_1 = 10$, then V_1 will keep outperforming the other code versions for larger values of P_1.

The implication of the monotonicity assumption is that there is at most one cross-over point for each branch. The interval found using the method described above precisely models this behavior.

This simplifying assumption relies on the compiler choosing meaningful measures to distinguish between code versions. In other words, for a given branch B_i guarding V_i, the dynamic program value P_i should be a measure of how "good" V_i is, compared to the code versions further down the tuning tree. That, in turn, puts restrictions on what P_i should measure. In the context of incremental flattening, each P_i measures the degree of parallelism of the guarded code version, and thus the monotonicity assumption should hold according to the common wisdom of optimizing the amount of parallelism.

The monotonicity assumption is closely related to the structure of the tuning forest. The tuning forest built by incremental flattening, and tuned by our

```
1   let mapscan2 [k] (ns: []i32) (xs: [k]i32) : [k]i32 =
2       loop xs for n in ns do
3         let m = k / n
4         let xss': [m][n]i32 = unflatten m n xs
5         let xss =
6           map2(\(row: [n]i32) (i: i32) ->
7                   loop (row: [n]i32) for _ in 0 ..< 64 do
8                     let row' = map (+i) row
9                     in scan (+) 0 row'
10              )
11              xss' (0 ..< m)
12        in flatten_to k xss
```

Fig. 7. Futhark program with size-variant parallelism.

technique, does not allow for more complex ways to discriminate between code versions. For instance, in Fig. 5, it is not possible to specify that V_1 should be preferred when $P_1 \leq 10$ or $P_1 \geq 100$, or that V_1 should be preferred when $P_1 \geq 10$ unless $P_2 \geq 100$. However, in principle, one can still model such casses by instructing the compiler to generate the code versions in a different order, or even to duplicate some code versions in the tuning forest. For instance Fig. 6a shows a reordered version of Fig. 1, which enables us to model the first restriction while still conforming with the monotonicity assumption. Similarly, the second restriction can be modeled by adding duplicate code versions, as in Fig. 6b, where V_1' and V_1'' are obtained from handicapping V_1 in the case when $P_1 < 10$ and $P_1 > 100$, respectively. Such transformations hint that the monotonicity restriction can be relaxed to a piece-wise monotonic one.

While our tuning technique is primarily aimed at incremental-flattening analysis, it should work in other contexts, as long as the modeled (dynamic) program property conforms with the monotonicity assumption.

3.5 Tuning Size-Variant Thresholds

In Sect. 3.3, we assumed that the degrees of parallelism exhibited by the different branches were constant during a single execution of the program. However, that is not always the case.

For instance, the mapscan2 function shown in Fig. 7 is *size-variant*. Again, we're not interested in the specific computation, but rather in the structure which serves to illustrate the difference between size-invariant and size-variant programs. The core algorithm is similar to mapscan1, but with a loop added around it. In each iteration of the outer loop, the input is transformed into a differently shaped matrix,[9] which is then mapped over. If Fig. 1 is the tuning tree for this function, P_1 and P_2 would take on different values during the course

---

[9] The unflatten function transforms an array into a matrix of the given dimensions. flatten transforms a matrix into an array.

```
1: function TUNEVARTHRESHOLD(p, d, t̄, i, bestRun)
2:     ePar' = ePar₁, ..., ePar_m ← EXPLOITEDPAR(p, d, t_i)
3:            ePar' is a sorted sequence of unique values
4:     ePar ← 0, ePar', ∞
5:     low  ← 0,      r_low  ← run p on d with t_i set to 0
6:     high ← m + 1, r_high ← bestRun
7:     (bestRun, bestInd) ← minInd(r_low, low, r_high, high)
8:     while low < high do
9:         mid ← ⌊(low + high)/2⌋
10:        r_mid ← run p on d with t_i set to ePar_mid
11:        if r_high was faster than r_mid then
12:            low ← mid + 1
13:        else
14:            if r_low was faster than r_mid then
15:                high ← mid - 1
16:            else
17:                r_grd ← run p on d with t_i set to ePar_{mid+1}
18:                if r_mid was faster than r_grd then
19:                    update bestRun, bestInd
20:                    high ← mid - 1
21:                else
22:                    update bestRun, bestInd
23:                    low ← mid + 2
24:                end if
25:            end if
26:        end if
27:    end while
28:    (lb_i, ub_i) ← expand bestInd to left and right
29:                within a given runtime variance
30:    return ((lb_i, ub_i), bestRun)
31: end function
```

Fig. 8. Tuning algorithm for a size-variant threshold. $\overline{ePar'}$ is a sorted sequence of unique values denoting the amount of parallelism of the code version guarded by threshold t_i, encountered during the execution of dataset d.

of a single execution, because the degrees of outer and inner parallelism (as determined by the size of the matrix) change.

It follows that when tuning a single threshold on a single dataset, it is no longer the case that the guard predicate should always be either true or false. For instance, if a given dynamic program value P_i takes on the values 10, 50, and 100 during a single execution, it might be optimal to run V_i when P_i is 100, but otherwise choose the best code version further down the tree. However, according to the monotonicity assumption, there will still be a single cross-over point for size-variant thresholds, so it is still possible to find an optimal interval for a single dataset. The question is, how do we do that efficiently.

The answer relies on the insight that only the exhibited dynamic program values and ∞ are relevant to try as threshold values, as these are the only values that accurately discriminate between different distributions of code versions. In the example from above, there are four possible ways to distribute the loop iterations: Setting T_i to 10 will always choose V_i, setting T_i to 50 will choose V_i except when P_i is 10, and so on. Any other value, like 45, will not result in changes in what code versions are being run. Therefore, we only have to try those particular values.

Furthermore, the monotonicity assumption implies that there is a gradient in the direction of the optimal solution, so we can actually perform a binary search in the space of possible threshold values, by trying two neighboring threshold candidates and determining the gradient in order to reduce the search space.

Figure 8 shows an alternate version of TUNETHRESHOLD which is used to tune size-variant thresholds using this binary tuning technique. Using this function, we can tune one size-variant thresholds on a single dataset in $O(\log n)$ runs, where n is the number of different degrees of parallelism exhibited.

We conclude with a formal argument of why the use of gradient is sound under the monotonic assumption. We denote by V_i a code version that corresponds to a size-variant threshold T_i whose dynamic program property takes n distinct increasingly-sorted values $P_i^{1\cdots n}$ during the execution on a fixed dataset d. We denote by V'_{i+1} the near-optimal subprogram to the right of the branch. Assume we have run the program with $T_i \leftarrow P_i^j$ and with $T_i \leftarrow P_i^{j+1}$ and that the first run is faster. The only difference between the two runs is that the first run uses V_i for dynamic property value P_i^j while the second run uses V'_{i+1} for P_i^j; the other uses of code versions V_i and V'_{i+1} are the same between the two runs.

The first run being faster thus means that V_i is faster than V'_{i+1} for the dynamic value P_i^j, and by the monotonic assumption, it follows that it will remain faster for any value higher than P_i^j, which means that we should continue the binary search to the left of P_i^j (lines 19–20 in Fig. 8). Conversely, following a similar logic, if the second run is faster, then we should continue the binary search to the right of P_i^j (lines 22–23 in Fig. 8).

4   Experimental Validation

This section evaluates the tuning time of our technique as well as the performance of the tuned programs (i.e., the accuracy of tuning), by comparing with results obtained using the old OpenTuner-based black-box tuner. All benchmarks are tuned and run on a GeForce RTX 2080Ti GPU, though we have observed similar results on an older GTX780Ti.

We use a set of publicly available, non-trivial benchmarks and datasets. For each benchmark, we base our analysis on two datasets, chosen to exhibit different degrees of parallelism and to prefer different code versions. The benchmarks, datasets and the number of thresholds are shown in Table 1. Heston and BFAST are real-world applications: Heston is a calibration program for the Hybrid Stochastic Local Volatility/Hull-White model [16], for which we use datasets from the `futhark-benchmarks` repository[10]. BFAST [14] is used to

---

[10] https://github.com/diku-dk/futhark-benchmarks.

Table 1. Tuning-time speedup between the OpenTuner implementation and our auto-tuner on a number of benchmarks on GeForce RTX 2080 Ti. There are two datasets for each benchmark, D1 and D2, with dataset sizes given in their respective columns. The LUD benchmark is size-variant, the rest are size-invariant.

Benchmark	D1	D2	# Thrs.	Opent.	Our	Speedup
Heston	1062 quotes	10000 quotes	9	3798 s	168 s	22.59x
BFAST	peru	Africa	16	1127 s	206 s	5.47x
LocVolCalib	Medium	Large	2	101 s	21 s	4.83x
OptionPricing	Small	Large	1	31 s	6 s	5.40x
LUD	$\mathcal{M}^{256 \times 256}$	$\mathcal{M}^{2048 \times 2048}$	9	611 s	430 s	1.42x
Backprop	2^{14}	2^{20}	1	30 s	8 s	3.65x
LavaMD	$\mathcal{M}^{10^3 \times 50}$	$\mathcal{M}^{3^3 \times 50}$	4	104 s	28 s	3.67x
NW	$\mathcal{M}^{2048 \times 2048}$	$\mathcal{M}^{1024 \times 1024}$	6	222 s	29 s	7.62x
NN	1×855280	4096×128	3	125 s	36 s	3.48x
SRAD	$1 \times \mathcal{M}^{502 \times 458}$	$1024 \times \mathcal{M}^{16 \times 16}$	4	148 s	28 s	5.31x
Pathfinder	$1 \times \mathcal{M}^{100 \times 10^5}$	$391 \times \mathcal{M}^{100 \times 256}$	1	66 s	10 s	6.81x

detect landscape changes, such as deforestation, in satellite time series data and is widely used by the remote sensing community. We use the peru and africa datasets from the `futhark-kdd19` repository[11].

LocVolCalib (local volatilty calibration) and OptionPricing are implementations of real-world financial computations from FinPar [3,20], for which we use datasets from the `finpar` repository[12].

LUD, Backprop, LavaMD, NW, NN, SRAD and Pathfinder are Futhark implementations of benchmarks from the Rodinia benchmark suite [7]. Some Rodinia benchmarks, like Backprop, only has one default dataset (layer length equal to 2^{16}). In those cases we've created datasets that span the Rodinia inputs—e.g., layer length 2^{14} and 2^{20} for Backprop—otherwise we have used the Rodinia datasets directly. The NW, SRAD and Pathfinder benchmarks implement batched versions of their respective algorithms, so the outer number is the number of matrix inputs ($\mathcal{M}$ denotes matrix). For instance, SRAD solves one instance of an image of size 502×458 for D1, and 1024 different images of sizes 16×16 for D2, while NN solves one nearest-neighbor problem for one query and 855280 reference points for D1, and 4096 problems each having 128 reference points.

We wish to investigate the impact of our tuning method on tuning time and run time using the tuned thresholds. Because the OpenTuner based tuner is inherently random, and benchmarking GPU programs is suspectible to run-time fluctuations, we base our analysis on three separate autotuning and benchmarking passes. For each pass, we first benchmark all programs untuned by run-

---

[11] https://github.com/diku-dk/futhark-kdd19.
[12] https://github.com/HIPERFIT/finpar.

ning them 500 times with each dataset, then we tune the programs using the OpenTuner-tool and benchmark all programs using the found thresholds (500 runs), and finally we tune using our autotuner and benchmark again (500 runs). We'll pick the best tuning times for both OpenTuner and our autotuner, but it should be noted that the OpenTuner-tool has a significantly larger variance in tuning time on some benchmarks, like LUD (between 366s and 881s). To measure run time performance we first find the fastest out of the 500 runs in each pass. Then, for OpenTuner, we will show both the best and worst of those three passes, while for our autotuner we will only show the worst, because the variance is significantly smaller (and our tuning strategy is deterministic otherwise). For OpenTuner, it is also important to point out that, because it was the only tool available to tune thresholds before creating the new autotuner, it has been highly optimized, and will, among other things, use memoization techniques to minimize the number of runs, i.e., it avoids running the same combination of code versions twice.

Table 1 shows the datasets used for each benchmark, the number of tuning thresholds[13] and the average tuning times using OpenTuner and our autotuner, as well as the speedup in tuning time. Overall, we see a significant reduction in tuning time, from 1.4x for LUD to 22.6x for Heston. Without those two outliers, the average speedup is 5.1x. In general, we see that more tuning parameters result in longer tuning times, but other factors also play in, such as the time it takes to run the benchmark on a single dataset and the number of different degrees of parallelism for each particular threshold. The LUD benchmark has the least improvement in tuning time: It has size-variant parallelism, so our autotuner has to perform more test runs to find the right thresholds. We'll see that OpenTuner sometimes finds bad threshold values for LUD, so the relatively small difference in tuning time should not necessarily be seen as a boon for OpenTuner.

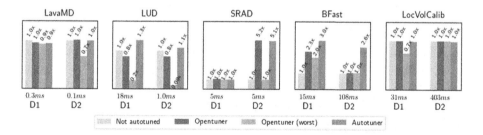

Fig. 9. Application run time speedup. The baseline is untuned performance. Higher is better.

Figure 9 shows the performance of five of the benchmarks described above: LavaMD, LUD, SRAD, BFAST and LocVolCalib. The rest of the benchmarks have similar performance characteristics when tuned using OpenTuner and our

---

[13] The number of code-versions is equal to the number of tuning thresholds plus one.

autotuner, primarily because of recent improvements in the default thresholds and heuristics used in the Futhark compiler. The benchmarks shown in Fig. 9 are interesting because the different tuning methods result in programs whose performance differ significantly.

LUD is an implementation of LU matrix diagonalization with size-variant parallelism, as mentioned above. Running this program efficiently is a matter of using intra-group parallelism as long as the inner parallelism fits inside a Cuda block, which is also what the untuned version does. Our autotuner correctly finds tuning parameters that encode this behavior while OpenTuner fails to do so. In fact, it sometimes produces extremely degenerate results, due to the randomness inherent in the technique.

In the SRAD benchmark, OpenTuner will sometimes find the correct threshold values the datasets, but not always, as shown in the second dataset. A similar story can be told for LocVolCalib and LavaMD, where the OpenTuner tool sometimes find bad threshold values.

BFAST, which also relies on intra-group parallelism and is highly sensitive to tuning parameter variations, receives a significant performance boost from accurate tuning. However, the OpenTuner tool cannot even handle the largest dataset for BFAST (africa) because it causes our GPU to run out of memory, with no suitable fallback strategy, which is why we see no improvement in the second dataset at all compared to the untuned version. Our autotuner can correctly identify which threshold is causing the device to run out of memory and correctly tune to avoid it.

Interestingly, one can observe that benchmarks which have many thresholds, but not a big difference in tuning time, such as LUD and BFAST, are also the ones on which OpenTuner results in the worst program execution time. OpenTuner is not able to accurately discriminate between the different code versions, and seems to get stuck in local minimas because it terminates before the time-out is reached.

Finally, we should emphasize that, in contrast to the OpenTuner-based tool, the tuning time of our autotuner is deterministic. This means that you can reason about how many datasets you want to tune on, without having to fear tuning for unexpectedly long time. For instance, one might use the savings in tuning time to increase the set of training datasets, so as to improve the likelihood of hitting the threshold sweet spots, thus improving the prediction for new datasets.

5   Related Work

The study of autotuning solutions has been motivated by two observations: The first is that, in general, there might not exist one optimization recipe that results in best performance across all datasets, i.e., "one size does not fit all". The second is that not all performance optimizations are portable across different hardware combinations. Related work is aligned along three directions:

The first direction is to infer the best configuration of compilation flags that results in the *best average performance* across a set of training datasets on a given hardware setup. Solutions typically apply machine learning techniques, for example by relying on supervised off-line training [13], and promising results have been reported for both multi-core [8] and many-core [5] systems. For example, such techniques have successfully inferred (i) the compilation flags of the -O3 GCC option, and improved on it when the set of programs is restricted, and (ii) near-optimal tile sizes used in GPU code generation of linear algebra operations that outperformed finely-tuned libraries, such as cuBLAS.

The second direction has been to promote a compiler design reliant on autotuning that separates concerns: The compiler maintains a thesaurus of legal code transformations that might improve performance, and the autotuner is responsible for selecting the combination of transformations that maximize performance for *a given dataset run on some given hardware*. For example, Lift [15,27] and SPIRAL [12], exploit the rich rewrite-rule systems of functional languages in this way. Similarly, Halide [24] applies stochastic methods to find the best fusion schedule of image-processing pipelines, corresponding to various combinations of tiling, sliding window and work replication transformations. The per-dataset tuning is feasible in cases such as stencil computations, because the important tuning parameter is the stencil's shape, and the performance is likely portable on larger arrays.

The third research direction is to provide a general black-box autotuning framework such as OpenTuner [4], which uses a repertoire of stochastic search strategies, such as hill-climbing and simulated annealing, and also provides the means for the user to define custom search strategies. ATF [25] similarly follows this research direction and provides a generic framework that supports annotation-driven autotuning of programs written in any language. ATF simplifies the programming interface, allows the specification of constraints between tuning parameters and optimizes the process of search-space generation, but it only supports tuning a single dataset at a time. However, like OpenTuner, ATF does not use any knowledge of the program structure or of the compilation technique that is being used.

Such strategies can work well when every point in the space provides new information to guide the tuning. Unfortunately, our results indicate that the threshold parameter space of compilation schemes such as incremental flattening [19] is too sparse for such black-box startegies to be effective in practice: (i) in several cases, near-optimal configurations are not (reliably) found even when enough time is given for the search to finish naturally, and (ii) typically the tuning times are too large (and unpredictable), which makes it infeasible to use it during application development stages.

The main high-level difference of our approach, compared to these other approaches, is that it integrates the multi-versioned compilation with a relatively cheap and one-time autotuning process that results in one executable that automatically selects the most efficient combination of code versions for *any* dataset.[14] In comparison, the first direction selects the compilation strategy that is best on average for the training datasets, and the second direction needs to repeat the autotuned compilation whenever the stencil shape changes.

At a very high level, our method has some relation to software product lines (SPLs), where techniques have been explored to, for instance, generate a multitude of code versions and statically determine the energy usage of each [9].

Finally, another related research direction has been the study of various run-time systems aimed at dynamically optimizing program execution on the target dataset, for example by dynamically adjusting the granularity at which parallelism is exploited for multicore execution [2,28] and by speculatively executing in parallel loops with statically unknown dependencies [10,21,23].

6   Conclusion

We have presented a general technique for tuning thresholds in multi-versioned programs. By taking advantage of the knowledge of the tuning-forest, we can efficiently target each code version in turn, thereby finding the (near-)optimal threshold parameters using only the necessary number of runs. For size-invariant branches, we only require a single test-run, whereas we perform a binary search across the set of unique threshold values for size-variant branches. Having tuned thresholds for each dataset individually, we combine the partial-tuning results at the end, in order to find threshold parameters that optimally distinguish between the code versions in question. We have shown substantial improvement in tuning time and tuned-execution run-time compared to the previous OpenTuner-based tuning technique. Furthermore, we remark that a significant amount of effort has been devoted to downgrade the incremental-flattening analysis by pruning at compile time the number of generated code versions, precisely because the OpenTuner-based autotuning was unreliable and slow.

In comparison with more complex stochastic-search strategies, our framework proposes a custom solution that trades off generality—each predicate introduces one unknown threshold, and thus there might not exist a set of threshold values that optimally implements a top-level strategy of combining code versions—for an efficient solution that significantly reduces the number of program runs. Finally, our strategy promotes human reasoning and understanding of results, by providing sanity-assumptions, limitations and guarantees:

– The central assumption is that the dynamic values that appear in the tuning predicates satisfy a notion of monotonic behavior, namely if version V_i is optimal for a certain P_i then it remains optimal for any dynamic value greater than P_i.

---

[14] This way of combining static and dynamic analysis by means of lightweight predicates is reminiscent of techniques used for automatic parallelization of sequential loops [22,26].

– The principal guarantee is that if a (near-)optimal set of threshold values exists then it will be found. If it does not exists then necessarily the intersection of threshold intervals across datasets is empty, and a reasonable approximation is derived by considering the maximal number of datasets that result in a non-empty intersection. Alternatively, user-defined attributes may in principle change the order in which code-versions are generated, which may enable the existence of an optimal configuration.

References

1. https://docs.nvidia.com/cuda/
2. Acar, U.A., Aksenov, V., Charguéraud, A., Rainey, M.: Provably and practically efficient granularity control. In: PPoPP 2019, pp. 214–228 (2019). https://doi.org/10.1145/3293883.3295725
3. Andreetta, C., et al.: FinPar: a parallel financial benchmark **13**(2) (2016). https://doi.org/10.1145/2898354
4. Ansel, J., et al.: OpenTuner: an extensible framework for program autotuning. In: International Conference on Parallel Architectures and Compilation Techniques (2014). http://groups.csail.mit.edu/commit/papers/2014/ansel-pact14-opentuner.pdf
5. Baghdadi, R., et al.: PENCIL: a platform-neutral compute intermediate language for accelerator programming. In: 2015 PACT, pp. 138–149 (2015)
6. Blelloch, G.E., Hardwick, J.C., Sipelstein, J., Zagha, M., Chatterjee, S.: Implementation of a portable nested data-parallel language. J. Parallel Distrib. Comput. **21**(1), 4–14 (1994)
7. Che, S., et al.: Rodinia: a benchmark suite for heterogeneous computing. In: IEEE International Symposium on Workload Characterization, 2009. IISWC 2009, pp. 44–54 (10 2009). https://doi.org/10.1109/IISWC.2009.5306797
8. Chen, Y., et al.: Evaluating iterative optimization across 1000 datasets. In: PLDI 2010, pp. 448–459. https://doi.org/10.1145/1806596.1806647
9. Couto, M., Borba, P., Cunha, J., Fernandes, J.P., Pereira, R., Saraiva, J.: Products go green: worst-case energy consumption in software product lines. In: Proceedings of the 21st International Systems and Software Product Line Conference, SPLC 2017, Volume A, Sevilla, Spain, 25–29 September 2017, pp. 84–93. https://doi.org/10.1145/3106195.3106214
10. Dang, F., Yu, H., Rauchwerger, L.: The R-LRPD test: speculative parallelization of partially parallel loops. In: Proceedings 16th International Parallel and Distributed Processing Symposium, pp. 20–29 (2002). https://doi.org/10.1109/IPDPS.2002.1015493
11. Elsman, M., Henriksen, T., Annenkov, D., Oancea, C.E.: Static interpretation of higher-order modules in Futhark: functional GPU programming in the large. Proc. ACM Program. Lang. **2**(ICFP), 97:1–97:30 (2018)
12. Franchetti, F., et al.: SPIRAL: extreme performance portability. Proc. IEEE **106**, 1935–1968 (2018)
13. Fursin, G., et al.: Milepost GCC: machine learning enabled self-tuning compiler. Int. J. Parallel Program. **39**, 296–327 (2011)
14. Gieseke, F., Rosca, S., Henriksen, T., Verbesselt, J., Oancea, C.E.: Massively-parallel change detection for satellite time series data with missing values. In: 2020 IEEE 36th International Conference on Data Engineering (ICDE), pp. 385–396 (2020). https://doi.org/10.1109/ICDE48307.2020.00040

15. Hagedorn, B., Stoltzfus, L., Steuwer, M., Gorlatch, S., Dubach, C.: High performance stencil code generation with lift. In: ACM, pp. 100–112 (2018). https://doi.org/10.1145/3168824

16. Henriksen, T., Elsman, M., Oancea, C.E.: Modular acceleration: tricky cases of functional high-performance computing. In: Proceedings of the 7th ACM SIGPLAN International Workshop on Functional High-Performance Computing, pp. 10–21. FHPC 2018 (2018). https://doi.org/10.1145/3264738.3264740

17. Henriksen, T., Hellfritzsch, S., Sadayappan, P., Oancea, C.: Compiling generalized histograms for GPU. In: Proceedings of the International Conference for High Performance Computing, Networking, Storage and Analysis. SC 2020. IEEE Press (2020)

18. Henriksen, T., Serup, N.G.W., Elsman, M., Henglein, F., Oancea, C.E.: Futhark: purely functional GPU-programming with nested parallelism and in-place array updates. In: PLDI 2017, pp. 556–571 (2017). https://doi.org/10.1145/3062341.3062354

19. Henriksen, T., Thorøe, F., Elsman, M., Oancea, C.: Incremental flattening for nested data parallelism. In: PPoPP 2019, pp. 53–67. https://doi.org/10.1145/3293883.3295707

20. Oancea, C.E., Andreetta, C., Berthold, J., Frisch, A., Henglein, F.: Financial software on GPUs: between Haskell and Fortran. In: Proceedings of the 1st ACM SIGPLAN Workshop on Functional High-Performance Computing, FHPC 2012, pp. 61–72 (2012). https://doi.org/10.1145/2364474.2364484

21. Oancea, C.E., Mycroft, A.: Set-congruence dynamic analysis for thread-level speculation (TLS). In: Amaral, J.N. (ed.) LCPC 2008. LNCS, vol. 5335, pp. 156–171. Springer, Heidelberg (2008). https://doi.org/10.1007/978-3-540-89740-8_11

22. Oancea, C.E., Rauchwerger, L.: A hybrid approach to proving memory reference monotonicity. In: Rajopadhye, S., Mills Strout, M. (eds.) LCPC 2011. LNCS, vol. 7146, pp. 61–75. Springer, Heidelberg (2013). https://doi.org/10.1007/978-3-642-36036-7_5

23. Oancea, C.E., Selby, J.W.A., Giesbrecht, M., Watt, S.M.: Distributed models of thread-level speculation. In: Proceedings of International Conference on Parallel and Distributed Processing Techniques and Applications (PDPTA 2005), pp. 920–927 (2005)

24. Ragan-Kelley, J., Barnes, C., Adams, A., Paris, S., Durand, F., Amarasinghe, S.: Halide: a language and compiler for optimizing parallelism, locality, and recomputation in image processing pipelines. In: PLDI 2013, pp. 519–530. ACM (2013). https://doi.org/10.1145/2491956.2462176

25. Rasch, A., Gorlatch, S.: ATF: a generic directive-based auto-tuning framework. Concurrency Comput. Pract. Exp. **31**(5), e4423 (2019)

26. Rus, S., Hoeflinger, J., Rauchwerger, L.: Hybrid analysis: static & dynamic memory reference analysis. Int. J. Parallel Program. **31**(3), 251–283 (2003). https://doi.org/10.1023/A:1024597010150

27. Steuwer, M., Fensch, C., Lindley, S., Dubach, C.: Generating performance portable code using rewrite rules: from high-level functional expressions to high-performance OpenCL code. In: ICFP 2015, pp. 205–217. https://doi.org/10.1145/2784731.2784754

28. Thoman, P., Jordan, H., Fahringer, T.: Compiler multiversioning for automatic task granularity control. Concurrency Comput. Pract. Exp. **26**(14), 2367–2385 (2014). https://doi.org/10.1002/cpe.3302

A Generic Back-End for Exploratory Programming

Damian Frolich[1,2]($\boxtimes$) and L. Thomas van Binsbergen[2] (iD)

[1] Department of Computer Science, Vrije Universiteit, Amsterdam, The Netherlands
[2] Informatics Institute, University of Amsterdam, Amsterdam, The Netherlands
{dfrolich,ltvanbinsbergen}@acm.org

Abstract. Exploratory programming is a form of incremental program development in which the programmer can try and compare definitions, receives immediate feedback and can simultaneously experiment with the language, the program and input data. Read-Eval-Print-Loop interpreters (REPLs) and computational notebooks are popular tools for exploratory programming. However, their usability, capabilities and user-friendliness are strongly dependent on the underlying interpreter and, in particular, on the ad hoc engineering required to ready the underlying interpreter for incremental program development. To break this dependency, this paper adopts a principled approach and implements a so-called exploring interpreter as a back-end to support various development environments for exploratory programming.

This paper contributes by presenting a generic Haskell implementation of the exploring interpreter – applicable to a large class of software languages – and demonstrates its usage to develop a variety of interfaces with a shared back-end, including command-line REPLs, computational notebooks and servers with reactive APIs. The design of the back-end is evaluated by defining a variety of interfaces for existing languages, including eFLINT, a domain-specific language for normative reasoning, and Funcons-beta, the language developed by the PLanCompS project to enable component-based operational semantics.

Keywords: Interpreters · Development environments · Operational semantics · Read-Eval-Print · Definitional interpreters

1 Introduction

Read-Eval-Print-Loop interpreters (REPLs) provide an alternative form of programming to the traditional compile-edit-run cycle. Popular examples of REPLs include JShell for Java, IPython for Python, PsySH for PHP and GHCi for Haskell, which are either part of the language's distribution (JShell and GHCi) or provide additional features on top of the REPL of the distribution (IPython and PsySH). REPLs enable an incremental form of programming in which a program is developed as a sequence of smaller programs executed one-by-one with immediate feedback after every (intermediate) program. This feedback typically

© Springer Nature Switzerland AG 2021
V. Zsók and J. Hughes (Eds.): TFP 2021, LNCS 12834, pp. 24–43, 2021.
https://doi.org/10.1007/978-3-030-83978-9_2

includes the value computed by the program (in case of an expression) and a summary on the (side-)effects of the program, enabling the programmer to update their mental model of the REPLs underlying state. An example interaction with JShell is shown in Fig. 1a.

```
jshell> int x;
x ==> 0
jshell>
   class A {
     public void run() { x++; }
   }
|  created class A
jshell> A a = new A();
a ==> A@5ce65a89
jshell> a.run()
jshell> x
x ==> 1
```

(a) JShell interaction.

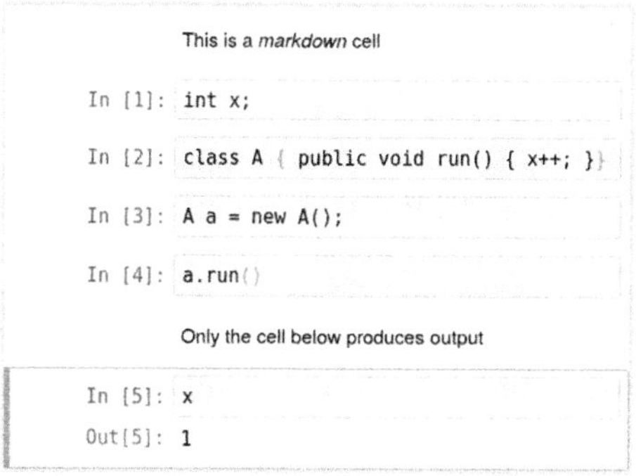

```
                         This is a markdown cell
In [1]:  int x;
In [2]:  class A { public void run() { x++; }}
In [3]:  A a = new A();
In [4]:  a.run()
                    Only the cell below produces output
In [5]:  x
Out[5]:  1
```

(b) IJava interaction.

Fig. 1. Example interactions in JShell and IJava.

This quicker form of interaction, compared to the compile-edit-run cycle, makes REPLs more suitable for quickly testing library functions, retrieving (type) information on available bindings, experimenting with definitions, debugging, and analysing data. However, data analysts and other domain-experts, not necessarily skilled in software engineering, prefer to use computational notebooks for these tasks [32, 41]. Computational notebooks are documents consisting of a sequence of three types of cells: code cells, output cells and prose (or documentation) cells. Popular examples are Mathematica [13] and the notebooks built using the Jupyter platform [18]. Code cells are executed one-by-one, with output displayed in output cells, thereby supporting the same kind of incremental program development as REPLs. This is reflected in the design of the Jupyter platform, wherein Python notebooks use the IPython REPL internally [18]. An example of a Jupyter IJava notebook (based on JShell) is given in Fig. 1b.

REPLs and (Jupyter) notebooks require significant engineering, especially for languages, such as Java and to a lesser extent Haskell, that do not naturally support incremental program development. For example, the code fragments in Fig. 1 can be recognised as Java code but they do not form a valid Java program individually nor as a sequence. JShell can be seen as implementing an extension of Java rather than Java itself. However, the precise details of this extension – its syntax and semantics – are not clearly specified and are not part of the Java documentation. Moreover, as Fig. 1 demonstrates, JShell and IJava are not consistent in how they present output. In the example, JShell produces detailed information about the effects of most code fragments whereas IJava only produces output for the last code fragment, revealing a difference between both tools in how they treat computed values and (side-)effects which, one could argue, are matters of language semantics rather than tool implementation.

In previous work [8], a principled approach is proposed for implementing REPLs, and other interfaces for incremental programming, using language engineering techniques to explicitly define language extensions, thereby clarifying the difference between the base language and the language implemented by the REPL. The approach makes it possible to develop generic interfaces which under the hood use a definitional interpreter[1] to execute programs. The approach further suggest the use of a so-called exploring interpreter on top of a definitional interpreter for *exploratory programming*. Exploratory programming is an open-ended form of incremental programming in which both the goal and the path towards the goal are discovered as part of the process [3,36,45]. The programmer discovers these through interactions with the underlying interpreter by testing definitions, evaluating expressions, analysing intermediate results and using backtracking to undo work and explore alternative directions.

1.1 Contributions

This paper contributes by presenting and discussing a generic implementation of the exploring interpreter algorithm of [8] in Haskell. The implementation is generic in the sense that it can be applied to large class of languages, including all languages that can have their semantics expressed by a transition function, for example in a transition system in the style of Plotkin [34].

Potential applications of the implemented algorithm are manifold. The genericity of the algorithm makes it possible to implement and experiment with features that benefit exploratory programming in a language-independent fashion. These features can then be used in a variety of interfaces and can be reused across languages. In other words, the exploring interpreter adds a level of indirection that makes it possible to deliver multiple programming interfaces for the same language by reusing the back-end and to deliver generic programming interfaces that can be reused across languages. Concretely, this paper:

- Presents a generic implementation of the exploring interpreter algorithm of [8] in Haskell and discusses the key design choices of the implementation
- Demonstrates the ability to reuse the algorithm as a back-end for various programming interfaces for exploratory programming and performs a qualitative evaluation on the implementation
- Applies the generic back-end to Funcons-beta [7] and eFLINT [6]. This effort made a significant, positive impact on the usability and applicability of these languages, demonstrating the practicality of the principled approach of [8]

This paper is organised as follows. Section 2 and 3 describe background and related work. Section 4 presents an initial implementation of the exploring interpreter algorithm. Section 5 applies the algorithm to the Funcons-beta

---

[1] A definitional interpreter for a language is an interpreter that simultaneously implements and defines the language's operational semantics, often defined in a meta-language or language workbench in the context of domain-specific languages.

and eFLINT languages, demonstrating several types of front-ends for exploratory programming. To support these various types of front-ends, the initial implementation is extended in several ways in Sect. 5 as part of a qualitative evaluation. Section 6 concludes.

2 Background

This section introduces the methodology and related concepts put forward in [8]. In the proposed methodology, the first step towards developing a REPL for a language is to extend that language to a variant which is in the class of *sequential languages* – the class of languages that naturally support incremental program development. The class of sequential languages is defined in [8] as follows:

Definition 1. *A language L is a structure $\langle P, \Gamma, \gamma^0, I \rangle$ with P a set of programs, Γ a set of configurations, $\gamma^0 \in \Gamma$ an initial configuration and I a definitional interpreter assigning to each program $p \in P$ a function $I_p : \Gamma \to \Gamma$.*

Definition 2. *A language $L = \langle P, \Gamma, \gamma^0, I \rangle$ is* sequential *if there is an operator $\otimes$ such that for every $p_1, p_2 \in P$ and $\gamma \in \Gamma$ it holds that $p_1 \otimes p_2 \in P$ and that $I_{p_1 \otimes p_2}(\gamma) = (I_{p_2} \circ I_{p_1})(\gamma)$.*

The chosen definition of languages captures all software language that can have their semantics expressed as a deterministic transition function and includes real-world, large-scale, deterministic programming languages – as demonstrated by the body of literature on big-step, small-step and natural semantics [1,15,24,26,34] – and does not exclude languages with non-deterministic aspects when these aspects can be captured algebraically [48]. Configurations capture all information necessary to determine the behaviour of a program. A definitional interpreter is described as assigning to each program an *effect* – a function over configurations. A sequential language is a language in which every sequence of programs is a valid program that has the same effect as the composition of the effects of the individual programs in the sequence.

As an example, consider a simple imperative language such as WHILE [1,5]. In [5], a transition system is defined to capture the semantics of WHILE commands. A configuration in this system contains a sequence of output values and a store to keep track of variable assignments. The system can be used to give a definitional interpreter for WHILE, as required by Definition 1, for which it is possible to prove that $I_{C_1; C_2}(\gamma) = (I_{C_2}; I_{C_1})(\gamma)$, i.e. to prove that WHILE is a sequential language according to Definition 2 by choosing ; for $\otimes$.

The central idea of the approach is that an interpreter for a sequential language can be used, without (further) modification, by the back-end of a REPL, as well as by other interfaces for incremental programming. In other words, a REPL is considered to be just one type of interface for programming in the style that is characteristic of REPLs. The precise behaviour of a programming interface is clarified by separating the task of building the interface into language engineering – producing a sequential variant of the base language and an interpreter – and the engineering required to link interface actions to the interpreter and to visualise the effects of programs.

The methodology further proposes the use of a so-called *exploring interpreter* to support exploratory programming. An exploring interpreter is a bookkeeping device on top of a definitional interpreter keeping track of executed programs and visited configurations. The **execute** action of an exploring interpreter for a language executes a program by applying the definitional interpreter for the language while keeping track of the encountered configurations and executed programs in an execution graph, reflecting the entire history of the current interactive session. The execution graph has configurations as nodes and edges between nodes are labelled with programs such that an edge between s and t labelled p indicates that executing p in the context of s yields t, i.e. $I_p(s) = t$. The **revert** action makes it possible to choose any (previously visited) configuration as providing the execution context for the next program, thereby enabling exploratory programming. If the language to which the generic algorithm is applied is a sequential language, then the execution graph of the resulting exploring interpreter is closed under transitivity. This property guarantees the soundness of a variety of operations on the graph.

3   Related Work

Definitional interpreters of the kind captured by Definition 1 can be produced in a language workbench [11] such as Spoofax [16] or the $\mathbb{K}$ framework [19], a meta-language such as Rascal [17], a suitable general-purpose language such as Haskell [14,23,30], or can be generated from a formal definition of the operational semantics of the language [2,7,42,47]. These tools and techniques have in common that the semantics of the object language are formulated in an existing (formal) language with well-understood, executable semantics. The first use of definitional interpreters is by Reynolds, employing them as a vehicle for analysing languages [37,38]. His analysis took advantage of the formal similarity between denotational and interpretative semantics [39]. Various approaches to formal semantics can be explained in terms of Initial Algebra Semantics [12] in which algebraic signatures denote the constructs of a language and semantics are expressed as algebras over signatures. Modular approaches have been developed that make it possible to extend languages with little or no overhead [44], such as monad transformers [21,25], algebraic effect handlers [33,49], entity propagation in Modular Structural Operational Semantics [2,26], and copy-rules and forwarding in Attribute Grammars [43,46]. These approaches greatly enhance the practice of defining and maintaining definitional interpreters. In modern general-purpose languages, we see advanced use of monads in Haskell [23,31], Object Algebras [29] in Java, C# and Scala and intrinsically-typed definitional interpreters in Agda [40].

The usage of an execution graph that contains all configurations produced through program execution is related to back-in-time debugging [9,20,22,35], in which programmers can go 'back in execution history'. The execution graph, however, captures all components required to reconstruct the full interactive session as it also records the executed programs.

Jupyter is an open-source project for bringing web-based computational notebooks to a wide audience [18]. The Jupyter platform provides a protocol for connecting notebooks to the language kernels, such as IPython and IJava, that take care of program execution. Jupyter is popular and the community supports a large number and wide variety of languages. Within the Jupyter platform, the exploring interpreter algorithm can serve as a layer on top of language kernels to improve support for exploratory programming within Jupyter notebooks.

4   Implementation

This section presents and discusses a generic implementation of the exploring interpreter algorithm of [8] in Haskell using a WHILE language as an example.

```
data Command = Seq Command Command
             |  Assign String Expr
             |  Print Expr
             |  While Expr Command
             |  Skip
data Expr       = Leq Expr Expr | Plus Expr Expr | LitExpr Literal | Id String
data Literal    = LitBool Bool | LitInt Integer

whileInterpreter :: Command → Config → Config
data Config     = Config { cfgStore :: Store, cfgOutput :: Output }
type Store      = Map String Literal
type Output     = [String]
initialConfig   = Config { cfgStore = empty, cfgOutput = [] }
```

The definitions of *Command*, *Config*, *initialConfig* and *whileInterpreter* form a language according to Definition 1. The definitional interpreter (not shown) uses configurations with lists of strings as output and stores to record assignments.

An exploring interpreter is implemented as a parameterized data type, where the type parameters denote the programs and configurations of a given language:

```
data Explorer p c = Explorer { defInterp    :: p → c → c
                            , config        :: c
                            , execEnv       :: Gr Ref p
                            , currRef       :: Ref
                            , genRef        :: Ref
                            , cmap          :: IntMap c
                            , sharing       :: Bool
                            , backTracking :: Bool }
```

The *defInterp* field holds the interpreter responsible for executing programs. The *config* field stores the current configuration, i.e. the configuration to be used for the execution context of the next program. The *execEnv* field holds the current execution graph and is implemented as an edge-labelled graph using the `fgl` library[2]. Edges are labelled by programs. The nodes of the execution graph are references (of type *Ref*) to configurations rather than actual configurations. References are implemented as integers and every new configuration gets a unique reference from an increasing counter (using *currRef* and *genRef*). The field *cmap* records the configuration to which each existing reference refers. The field *sharing* determines whether to detect that a configuration has been reached that has already been encountered in which case no fresh reference is generated. With sharing, a configuration is referred to by at most one reference and a node in the execution graph may have multiple incoming edges. Without sharing, multiple references may refer to the same configuration and each node of the execution graph has at most one incoming edge, i.e. the execution graph forms a tree. The *backTracking* field indicates whether a revert action is destructive and deletes nodes and edges.

A smart constructor is defined that, given a definitional interpreter and an initial configuration, produces an *Explorer*.

$$mkExplorer :: Bool \rightarrow Bool \rightarrow (p \rightarrow c \rightarrow c) \rightarrow c \rightarrow Explorer\ p\ c$$
$$mkExplorer\ share\ backtrack\ interpreter\ conf = Explorer$$

```
{ sharing      = share
, backTracking = backtrack
, defInterp    = interpreter
, config       = conf
, genRef       = 1
, currRef      = 1
, cmap         = IntMap.fromList [(1, conf)]
, execEnv      = mkGraph [(1, 1)] []}
mkExplorerStack = mkExplorer False True
mkExplorerTree  = mkExplorer False False
mkExplorerGraph = mkExplorer True False
```

The smart constructor has additional parameters to determine whether the constructed *Explorer* should apply sharing and (destructive) backtracking. Additional smart constructors are defined that construct *Explorer* variants based on different choices for the *share* and *backtrack* parameters. Without sharing and with destructive reverts, the execution graph forms a linked list with stack-like operations. Without sharing and without destructive revert, the execution graph forms a tree. Section 5 discusses these properties further.

An *Explorer* for the WHILE language can then be obtained as follows:

```
type WhileExplorer = Explorer Command Config
whileTree = mkExplorerTree whileInterpreter initialConfig
```

The exploring interpreter algorithm of [8] describes three actions that can be performed on exploring interpreters: **execute, revert** and **display** for executing programs, reverting to previous configurations and displaying the execution graph.

The **execute** action applies the underlying interpreter on a given program to transition from the current configuration to a (possibly new) configuration.

---
[2] https://hackage.haskell.org/package/fgl.

$execute :: (Eq\ c, Eq\ p) \Rightarrow p \rightarrow Explorer\ p\ c \rightarrow Explorer\ p\ c$
$execute\ p\ e = updateConf\ e\ (p, defInterp\ e\ p\ (config\ e))$

$updateConf :: (Eq\ c, Eq\ p) \Rightarrow Explorer\ p\ c \rightarrow (p, c) \rightarrow Explorer\ p\ c$
$updateConf\ e\ (p, newconf) =$
  if $sharing\ e$
    then case $findRef\ e\ newconf$ **of**
      $Just\ (r, \_) \rightarrow$
        if $hasLEdge\ (execEnv\ e)\ (currRef\ e, r, p)$
          then e $\{ config = newconf, currRef = r \}$
          else e $\{ config = newconf, currRef = r$
                    $, execEnv = insEdge\ (currRef\ e, r, p)\ (execEnv\ e) \}$
      $Nothing \rightarrow addNewPath\ e\ p\ newconf$
    else $addNewPath\ e\ p\ newconf$

The resulting configuration becomes the current configuration and the *Explorer* components are updated. If sharing is disabled, a configuration is always seen as unique and a new reference is created, the configuration is added to the execution graph, an edge from the original configuration to the new configuration is created, and the association between the new reference and configuration is stored. However, if sharing is enabled and the resulting configuration has already been encountered, then the previously assigned reference is used as the target of the new edge.

The **revert** operation takes a reference and changes the current configuration to the configuration matching the reference:

$revert :: Explorer\ p\ c \rightarrow Ref \rightarrow Maybe\ (Explorer\ p\ c)$
$revert\ e\ r =$ **case** $IntMap.lookup\ r\ (cmap\ e)$ **of**
        $Just\ c\ |\ backTracking\ e \rightarrow Just\ e\ \{ execEnv = execEnv', config = c$
                         $, cmap = cmap', currRef = r \}$
              $|\ otherwise$ $\rightarrow Just\ e\ \{ currRef = r, config = c \}$
      $Nothing$ $\rightarrow Nothing$
  where
    $nodesToDel = reachable\ r\ (execEnv\ e) \setminus\setminus [r]$
    $edgesToDel = filter\ toDel\ (edges\ (execEnv\ e))$
                 where $toDel\ (s, t) = s \in nodesToDel \lor t \in nodesToDel$
    $execEnv'$ $= (delEdges\ edgesToDel \circ delNodes\ nodesToDel)\ (execEnv\ e)$
    $cmap'$ $= deleteMap\ nodesToDel\ (cmap\ e)$

If a reference is given without a corresponding configuration, Nothing is returned. If there is a corresponding configuration, then the current reference is changed to the given reference and the current configuration is updated accordingly. Further behaviour of **revert** is determined by the *backTracking* field, indicating whether the action is destructive. If it is destructive, then all nodes and edges reachable from the given reference are removed from the execution graph.

Operation **display** produces a structured representation of the execution graph, with the current configuration highlighted. The goal of the display function is to allow interfaces to display and export (parts of) the graph, e.g. to provide an overview, selecting nodes to revert to and saving sessions for later reproduction. To accommodate a wide variety of interfaces, we export several

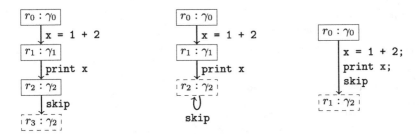

Fig. 2. Execution graphs after executing the WHILE commands x = 1 + 2, print x, and skip without and with sharing, and as a single command respectively. The current node is dashed. The notation $r : \gamma$ denotes a node labelled with reference r referring to configuration γ.

functions for accessing (parts of) the execution graph. For example, to access the entire execution graph, we export the following function:

$$executionGraph :: Explorer\ p\ c \rightarrow (Ref, [Ref], [((Ref, c), p, (Ref, c))])$$

The result contains the current node, a list of all nodes and a list of all edges in the execution graph. The edges contain both the reference and the referenced configuration of a node.

To obtain only part of the execution graph we export the following functions:

$$getTrace\ :: Explorer\ p\ c \rightarrow [((Ref, c), p, (Ref, c))]$$
$$getTraces :: Explorer\ p\ c \rightarrow [[((Ref, c), p, (Ref, c))]]$$

These functions provide one or multiple paths – referred to as traces – from the root node to the current node. As discussed in more detail in the next section, a node might have more than one trace (only) when sharing is enabled.

As an example of using exploring interpreters, consider the following sequence of WHILE commands: x = 1 + 2; print x; skip. Figure 2 shows the execution graph (with and without sharing) produced when each command in this sequence is executed individually by the exploring interpreter. The first commands adds the assignment of literal 3 to identifier x to the store and gives rise to the node with reference r_1. The second extends the output in the configuration with the literal 3, resulting in the node with reference r_2. The skip command has no effect on the configuration. Without sharing a new reference is created nonetheless (reference r_3 on the left of Fig. 2). With sharing a self-edge labelled with skip is created at the node with reference r_2 (middle of Fig. 2).

Folding and Unfolding Sequences. The sequence x = 1 + 2; print x; skip can also be executed as a single command, resulting in a single edge from r_0 to r_1 (right of Fig. 2). Because WHILE is a sequential language, both interpretations are equivalent in that they yield the same final configuration (γ_2). However, as shown by Fig. 2, the resulting execution graphs differ significantly, and, depending on the situation, one execution graph might be preferred over the other.

Some interfaces might let the programmer determine which execution is chosen. The following function is introduced to offer the flexibility of choice:

$$executeAll :: (Eq\ c, Eq\ p) \Rightarrow [p] \rightarrow Explorer\ p\ c \rightarrow Explorer\ p\ c$$
$$executeAll = flip\ (foldl\ \$\ flip\ execute)$$

If a program is a sequence of multiple programs to be executed individually, then the program can be unfolded to produce a list of programs. Conversely, if a list of programs is to be executed as a single program, the list can be folded.

5   Evaluation

In this section, we apply our implementation to two languages – eFLINT and Funcons-beta – and use the resulting specialised exploring interpreters to perform a qualitative evaluation on the generic implementation. The evaluation investigates the impact of destructive backtracking and sharing on the interactions with the execution graph. The result is a discussion on various aspects of exploratory programming, including exploratory programming styles, handling input/output and reproducibility. As part of the evaluation, several extensions to the implementation of the previous section are discussed. The basic and extended implementations are available on Hackage[3]. The specialised exploring interpreters for eFLINT[4] and Funcons-beta[5] are also available online.

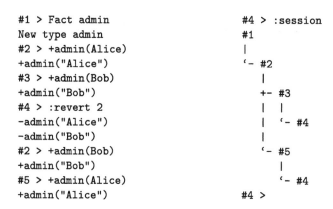

Fig. 3. A session in the command-line REPL for eFLINT.

The eFLINT language is a domain-specific language (DSL) for formalising norms from a variety of sources such as contracts, regulations and business policies [6]. The language currently has three main uses: exploring a policy specification in order to extend it or improve its internal consistency, statically assessing concrete scenarios for compliance, and dynamically enforcing norms in, and

---

[3] https://hackage.haskell.org/package/exploring-interpreters.
[4] https://gitlab.com/eflint/haskell-implementation.
[5] https://github.com/plancomps/funcons-tools.

assessing the compliance of, (distributed) software systems. The eFLINT language comes with three interfaces to support these tasks, each built on top of the exploring interpreter for the language: a command-line REPL, a web-interface and a TCP server. The language has been extended to a sequential variant by applying the methodology of [8] and the resulting definitional interpreter is used to specialize the generic exploring interpreter developed in this paper. Figure 3 shows a simple interaction with the command-line REPL in which a fact-type admin is introduced to record admin rights of users. The command-line REPL uses non-destructive reverts and sharing. A configuration contains a knowledge base of facts and after every **execute** and **revert** action the effects on the knowledge base are shown. The :session command shows all the traces in the execution graph in the form of a tree.

Figure 4 shows a part of the eFLINT web-interface in which a single trace is displayed (obtained via *getTrace*). The web-interface uses destructive backtracking and does not use sharing. The current node therefore has exactly one trace. The back-end is provided by a HTTP server built on top of the TCP server. The web-interface is used by first loading a specification file and then submitting a scenario – a sequence of statements and queries – for execution (using the 'Send phrase' button). The effects of statements and queries are shown in green and orange in the displayed trace. Violations are shown in red. A state can be expanded (state 8 in the example) to show the contents of the knowledge base and the last statement in the scenario that produced this state. The buttons below state 8 allow the trace to be updated in various ways by translating button-clicks to combinations of **execute** and **revert** actions.

The TCP server is also used to integrate the specialised exploring interpreter as a reasoning engine in multi-agent and service-oriented systems. Components of such systems can interact with one or more instances of the exploring interpreter to learn dynamically about permissions, obligations and violations. As such, eFLINT can be used for dynamic policy enforcement and compliance checking.

The PLanCompS project[6] has identified an open-ended library of so-called fundamental constructs (funcons) that can be used to give a component-based semantics to languages across language paradigms [10,27]. The funcons have their semantics formally defined in I-MSOS [28] and their I-MSOS specifications are translated to micro-interpreters [5,7]. These micro-interpreters can be composed arbitrarily to form (definitional) interpreters for different funcon libraries. Funcons-beta is the language defined by the definitional interpreter formed by composing the micro-interpreters of the funcons in the published funcons library[7]. Figure 5 shows the command-line REPL for Funcons-beta built on top of the specialised exploring interpreter for the language. This exploring interpreter is the result of a small language extension in which Funcons-beta is defined as a sequential language using the *accumulate* funcon as the composition operator $\otimes$. As a result, bindings produced by executing one funcon term prop-

---

[6] http://plancomps.org.

[7] https://plancomps.github.io/CBS-beta/Funcons-beta/Funcons-Index/.

Fig. 4. A web-interface for eFLINT showing (part of) a trace. State 8 is expanded.

agate to the next. The first funcon term executed in Fig. 5 produces a binding
for the identifier `"input"`.

```
#1> bind("input", read)
> "Hello world"
#2> print(bound("input"))
Hello world
#2>
```

$r_1 : \gamma_1$
$\quad$ bind("input",read)
$r_2 : \gamma_2$
print(bound("input"))

Fig. 5. A session in the command-line REPL for Funcons-beta.

Applying the generic exploring interpreter of this paper to these languages
required in the order of 50 to 100 lines of Haskell code. In both cases the main
effort was defining the definitional interpreter as an extension of the existing
interpreter of the language, which involved carefully choosing the contents of
the propagated configuration and the method of handling output.

Handling Input/Output, Side-Effects and Errors. Following the definition of languages (Definition 1), the implementation of the previous section considers a
definitional interpreter as a pure function expressing the effects of a program
on an input configuration. This approach requires the *simulation* of input and
output. For example, output can be considered an ever-growing list of (string)
values stored in the configurations, as shown by the definitional interpreter for

WHILE in Sect. 4. This choice reduces the potential for sharing since sharing can only take place in between two print statements (discussed further below). Similarly, input can be considered an ever-shrinking list of (string) values with the original input set in the initial configuration.

In Funcons-beta, the *read* reads a value from standard-in as shown in Fig. 5. In this example, the program `print(bound("input"))` creates a self-edge because output is not part of the configuration and the program has no other effect. The Funcons-beta command-line REPL takes advantage of an implementation of the exploring interpreter algorithm in which the definitional interpreter can perform effectful computations in a monad, i.e. it has the type:

$$\mathit{defInterp} :: \mathit{Monad}\ m \Rightarrow \mathit{programs} \rightarrow \mathit{configs} \rightarrow m\ \mathit{configs}$$

The command-line REPL for Funcons-beta instantiates m to the IO monad for interacting with standard-in and standard-out.

The introduction of the monad component has additional advantages. In particular, the monad enables distinguishing between effects and side-effects, with side-effects not being recorded in the execution graph. However, side-effects influence the soundness of the wider approach as the implementation can no longer guarantee that executing a program p in the context of configuration γ yields the same result every time. This has a negative impact on the reproducibility of a session and on the soundness of certain graph operations and optimisations.

The execution trace of Fig. 4 shows output messages indicating the success of queries and the occurrence of violations. When an eFLINT code fragment is executed (via the 'Send phrase' button at the top), the trace can either be updated using DOM manipulation or the page can be refreshed in its entirety. Although not efficient, refreshing is a convenient way to ensure consistency between the front-end and the back-end, as the front-end is redrawn based on the state of the back-end. This then requires the back-end to record output in order to inform the front-end of the output of programs (such as the results of queries) without re-executing programs. To support the reproducibility of output, we have chosen to add an output component to the definitional interpreters:

$$\mathit{defInterp} :: (\mathit{Monad}\ m, \mathit{Monoid}\ \mathit{out}) \Rightarrow \mathit{programs} \rightarrow \mathit{configs} \rightarrow m\ (\mathit{configs}, \mathit{out})$$

In accordance with Modular Structural Operational Semantics (MSOS) [26, 28], we generalise output to the class of monoidal types, allowing output to concatenate in between executions. Any output produced by the definitional interpreter is stored on the edges of the execution graph, alongside the program producing that output. The updated definitions of *Explorer* and *execute* are as follows:

```
data Explorer p m c o where    -- using GADT extension
  Explorer :: (Eq p, Eq c, Monad m, Monoid o) ⇒
    { defInterp :: p → c → m (Maybe c, o), ...} → Explorer p m c o
```

```
execute :: (Eq c, Eq p, Monad m, Monoid o) ⇒
    p → Explorer p m c o → m (Explorer p m c o, o)
```

$execute\ p\ e = \textbf{do}\ (mcfg, o) \leftarrow defInterp\ e\ p\ (config\ e)$
$\qquad\qquad\textbf{case}\ mcfg\ \textbf{of}\ \ Just\ cfg \rightarrow return\ (updateConf\ e\ (p, cfg, o), o)$
$\qquad\qquad\qquad\qquad\quad Nothing \rightarrow return\ (e, o)$

As before, the *updateConf* function is responsible for the extension of the execution graph, now also storing the output on edges. The *Maybe* component of the definitional interpreter is added to support interpreters that may fail. If the definitional interpreter returns *Nothing*, then no changes are made to the execution graph. The interpreter for Funcons-beta fails due to runtime errors, e.g. caused by unbound identifiers. The interpreter for eFLINT performs type-checking to find typing errors and perform coercions. Both types of errors cause the interpreter to fail and yield error messages as part of the output.

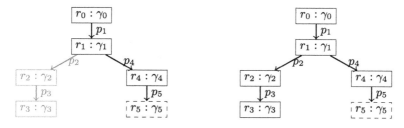

Fig. 6. Execution graph after execution p_1, p_2, p_3, reverting to r_1 and executing p_4, p_5. The gray nodes and edges are removed if the revert action is destructive.

Discussions on Backtracking. The decision to revert destructively by removing nodes and edges from the execution graph has practical and usability-related consequences. Non-destructive reverts enable a more powerful form of exploratory programming. Consider the two execution graphs in Fig. 6, created with and without destructive backtracking. The figure shows how destructive backtracking ensures that there is always exactly one node in the graph without outgoing edges. In other words, exploration always proceeds along a single path and a revert action always undoes the last n changes along that path (for some n). Conversely, when revert is not destructive, multiple paths are explored simultaneously and strategies like depth-first or breadth-first exploration are possible.

Destructive reverts save space by reducing the size of the execution graph. Applications in which multi-path exploration is not required should therefore be able to use destructive reverts. An example of such an application is the execution of a large test-suite in which all tests share a common prefix containing, for example, a number of declarations and initialisation statements. In this case, a programmer can execute all tests by executing the prefix once and subsequently executing all tests of the test-suite with backtracking in between tests to undo the changes of the previous test. Executing a test-suite this way can potentially save large amounts of time while the use of space is reduced with destructive reverts. Owing to the implementation presented in this paper, the eFLINT TCP server interface can be used to execute test-suites in the way described.

We conclude that both destructive and non-destructive reverts should be made available to the interface developer on a per application basis. In fact, we also make a version of *revert* available in which a parameter determines whether the revert is destructive as part of the function call. After all, even when multi-path exploration is desired, a programmer might still wish to undo programs.

Discussions on Sharing. The decision to apply sharing – i.e. ensuring that every configuration is referred to by at most one node – has significant impact on the practicality and usability of the exploring interpreter. The execution graph is more space-efficient with sharing rather than without, benefiting especially those applications in which output is not stored in configurations (see Fig. 5 and the discussion on output above). However, detecting opportunities for sharing is costly as it requires comparing (possibly many) configurations for equality. Our implementation determines that the type of configurations used by a language must be an instance of the *Eq* type-class. The *Eq*-instances derived by Haskell compilers use structural equality, a costly operation on large datastructures. Moreover, structural equality cannot be used when configurations store functions (such as continuations), in which case a custom equality instance is necessary. This is the case for Funcons-beta, in which a function for reading input (using either real or simulated input) is propagated throughout the definitional interpreter. As this function does not change in between calls to **execute**, it is safe to ignore the function when attempting sharing.

Besides space-efficiency, two further advantages of sharing can be observed. Firstly, through sharing, the exploring interpreter automatically detects the convergence of two exploration paths. In certain applications it will be insightful to the programmer to become aware of convergence. Similarly, sharing will detect cycles. The (abstract) execution graphs of Fig. 7 give examples of convergence (left) and a cycle (right). The session in Fig. 3 is a concrete instance of the graph showing convergence in Fig. 7. Note that by performing effects in a monad, the insights gained from convergence are reduced because convergence only concerns the effects represented by modifications to configurations.

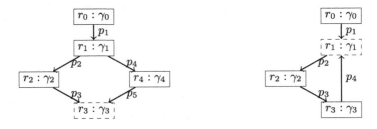

Fig. 7. Execution graphs showing convergence (left) and a cycle (right).

For the second example of a possible advantage of sharing, consider the situation in the graph on the right-hand side of Fig. 7 in which r_1 is the current node. If a program p_5 is to be executed next, and if p_5 is equivalent to p_2, then the exploring interpreter can recognise this and jump to r_2 without executing p_5 (but with adding the edge labelled p_5). If p_5 is a costly program to execute, considerable running time might be saved. This optimisation does not depend on sharing; the same situation could arise if the programmer reverted from r_3 to r_1 (without executing p_4 and without destructive backtracking). However, with sharing, opportunities to apply this optimisation are likely to increase in frequency. To further increase the potential of this optimisation it is beneficial to apply normalisation techniques to programs. The implementation and analysis of this optimisation is left as future work.

A disadvantages of sharing is that the revert action becomes ambiguous because, with sharing, a node can have more than one incoming edge and more than one trace. Selecting a node in the execution graph is not sufficient to revert to a particular moment in time with a unique history of prior actions. A possible solution is to retain a history of actions in the exploring interpreter. Similarly, it is unclear what the effect of a destructive revert should be in the context of sharing. In the current implementation, all outgoing paths of the new current node are removed from the execution graph[8]. Sharing also allows cycles that generate infinitely many paths with a repeated infix. These disadvantages demonstrate that sharing significantly complicates the execution graph in a way that makes it harder for the programmer to align their own mental model with the execution graph.

Although our implementation continues to support sharing, we expect that an exploring interpreter without sharing is sufficient for exploratory programming in many applications. This especially because even without sharing, convergent and cyclic exploration can still be detected by monitoring whether there are configurations referred to by more than one reference. Our implementation does not export a variant of *execute* with a parameter to determine whether to applying sharing. This is to preserve the aforementioned properties of the execution graph, e.g. that the execution graph forms a tree without sharing.

Saving and Loading Sessions. The execution graph of a pure exploring interpreter provides enough information to support the storing and reproduction of sessions generically. One possibility is to export the current configuration, giving the programmer the option to start a new session with the exported configuration as the initial configuration. To also record history, the path from the initial configuration to the current configuration can be exported (i.e. using *getTrace*). When sharing is enabled, all paths from the root node to the current node can be exported (using *getTraces*).

---

[8] With the exception of the node itself, in case of a cycle.

Exporting paths can be done in two ways, affecting in particular the size of the export and the costs of loading a session. The export can contain all components of the path – configurations, references, edges, programs and output – making it possible to load a session without executing programs. However, the soundness of this operation relies on the exploring interpreter being pure; if the programs of the saved session were executed in a monad, then there is no guarantee that the context provided by the monad is the same when the session is loaded (e.g. changes in database or file-system). Alternatively, space can be saved by exporting just the sequence of programs labelling the edges on the path. The session can then be loaded by executing this sequence of programs. Assuming the object-language is sequential, this sequence can be folded into a single program as part of the export or as part of loading the session (see the discussion on folding and unfolding in Sect. 4). Note that in this case, the export is a syntactically valid program that can also be executed with other implementations of the language (e.g. compilers and interpreters).

Finally, the execution graph can be exported in its entirety so that the entire session can be restored.

Discussion. In this section we have discussed several extensions to the implementation described in Sect. 4 and demonstrated the application of the generic back-end to develop several types of interfaces and applications. Based on this, we argue that the generic implementation can be applied widely. For example, we have made no assumptions about the style of (exploratory) programming provided by interfaces. This is demonstrated best by the various types of applications in which the same exploring interpreter for eFLINT is used. The back-end is also applicable to a large class of languages, including at least all languages that can have their semantics expressed as a (pure) transition function. This is best demonstrated by Funcons-beta, which captures the semantics of language constructs across paradigms such as functional programming, imperative programming, procedural programming, object-oriented programming and meta-programming [4]. Our implementation also ensures reproducibility, an important feature in notebooks [18,32]. In future work we wish to experiment with optimisations in the back-end and generic front-end components.

6   Conclusion

This paper presents a generic back-end for exploratory programming. The back-end is formed by the application of a generic exploring interpreter to a definitional interpreter for the chosen object language. The exploring interpreter adds a level of indirection that makes it possible to deliver multiple programming interfaces for the same language by reusing the back-end and to deliver generic programming interfaces that can be reused across languages. We have performed a qualitative evaluation on the implementation and demonstrated that the back-end can support various styles of exploratory programming, types of interfaces and types of applications such as command-line REPLs, computational notebooks and servers (e.g. to develop web-applications or multi-agent systems). The presented work marks just one step in a bigger research effort aimed at developing tooling and an infrastructure for the independent, modular and reusable design and implementation of programming interfaces for incremental programming and exploratory programming.

Acknowledgements. The work in this paper has been partially supported by the Kansen Voor West EFRO project (KVW00309) *AMdEX Fieldlab*, the NWO project (628.009.014) *Secure Scalable Policy-enforced Distributed Data Processing* (SSPDDP) and has been executed in a collaboration with the Agile Language Engineering (ALE) team (http://gemoc.org/ale/).

References

1. Astesiano, E.: Inductive and operational semantics. In: Neuhold, E., Paul, M. (eds.) IFIP State-of-the-Art Reports, Formal Descriptions of Programming Concepts, pp. 51–136. Springer (1991). ISBN: 978-3-540-53961-2
2. Bach Poulsen, C., Mosses, P.D.: Generating specialized interpreters for modular structural operational semantics. In: Gupta, G., Peña, R. (eds.) LOPSTR 2013. LNCS, vol. 8901, pp. 220–236. Springer, Cham (2014). https://doi.org/10.1007/978-3-319-14125-1_13
3. Beth Kery, M., Myers, B.A.: Exploring exploratory programming. In: 2017 IEEE Symposium on Visual Languages and Human-Centric Computing (VL/HCC), pp. 25–29 (2017). https://doi.org/10.1109/VLHCC.2017.8103446
4. van Binsbergen, L.T.: Funcons for HGMP: the fundamental constructs of homogeneous generative meta-programming (short paper). In: Proceedings of the 17th ACM SIGPLAN International Conference on Generative Programming: Concepts and Experience. GPCE 2018 (2018). https://doi.org/10.1145/3278122.3278132
5. van Binsbergen, L.T.: Executable Formal Specification of Programming Languages with Reusable Components. Ph.D. thesis, Royal Holloway, University of London (2019)
6. van Binsbergen, L.T., Liu, L., van Doesburg, R., van Engers, T.: eFLINT: a domain-specific language for executable norm specifications. In: Proceedings of the 19th ACM SIGPLAN International Conference on Generative Programming: Concepts and Experiences. GPCE 2020. ACM (2020)
7. van Binsbergen, L.T., Mosses, P.D., Sculthorpe, N.: Executable component-based semantics. J. Logical Algebraic Methods Program. **103**, 184–212 (2019). https://doi.org/10.1016/j.jlamp.2018.12.004
8. van Binsbergen, L.T., Verano Merino, M., Jeanjean, P., van der Storm, T., Combemale, B., Barais, O.: A Principled Approach to REPL Interpreters, pp. 84–100. ACM (2020). https://doi.org/10.1145/3426428.3426917
9. Bousse, E., Leroy, D., Combemale, B., Wimmer, M., Baudry, B.: Omniscient debugging for executable DSLs. J. Syst. Softw. **137**, 261–288 (2018)
10. Churchill, M., Mosses, P.D., Sculthorpe, N., Torrini, P.: Reusable components of semantic specifications. In: Transactions on Aspect-Oriented Software Development XII. TAOSD 2015, pp. 132–179 (2015)
11. Erdweg, S., et al.: Evaluating and comparing language workbenches: existing results and benchmarks for the future. Comput. Lang. Syst. Struct. **44**, 24–47 (2015)

12. Goguen, J.A., Thatcher, J.W., Wagner, E.G., Wright, J.B.: Initial algebra semantics and continuous algebras. J. ACM **24**(1), 68–95 (1977)
13. Hayes, B.: Thoughts on Mathematica. Pixel 1(January/February), pp. 28–34 (1990)
14. Hudak, P., Hughes, J., Peyton Jones, S., Wadler, P.: A history of haskell: being lazy with class. In: Proceedings of the Third ACM SIGPLAN Conference on History of Programming Languages. HOPL III. ACM (2007). https://doi.org/10.1145/1238844.1238856
15. Kahn, G.: Natural semantics. In: Proceedings of the 4th Annual Symposium on Theoretical Aspects of Computer Science. pp. 22–39. Springer-Verlag (1987)
16. Kats, L.C.L., Visser, E.: The Spoofax language workbench: Rules for declarative specification of languages and IDEs. In: International Conference on Object Oriented Programming Systems Languages and Applications. OOPSLA 2010, pp. 444–463. ACM (2010). https://doi.org/10.1145/1869459.1869497
17. Klint, P., Storm, T.v.d., Vinju, J.: Rascal: A domain specific language for source code analysis and manipulation. In: Proceedings of the 2009 Ninth IEEE International Working Conference on Source Code Analysis and Manipulation, pp. 168–177. IEEE Computer Society (2009). https://doi.org/10.1109/SCAM.2009.28
18. Kluyver, T., et al.: J development team: Jupyter notebooks - a publishing format for reproducible computational workflows. In: Loizides, F., Scmidt, B. (eds.) Positioning and Power in Academic Publishing: Players, Agents and Agendas, pp. 87–90. IOS Press, Netherlands (2016). https://doi.org/10.3233/978-1-61499-649-1-87
19. Lazar, D., et al.: Executing formal semantics with the $\mathbb{K}$ tool. In: Giannakopoulou, D., Méry, D. (eds.) FM 2012. LNCS, vol. 7436, pp. 267–271. Springer, Heidelberg (2012). https://doi.org/10.1007/978-3-642-32759-9_23
20. Lewis, B.: Debugging backwards in time. Computing Research Repository cs.SE/0310016 (2003). http://arxiv.org/abs/cs/0310016
21. Liang, S., Hudak, P., Jones, M.: Monad transformers and modular interpreters. In: 22nd Symposium on Principles of Programming Languages, pp. 333–343. ACM (1995)
22. Lienhard, A., Gîrba, T., Nierstrasz, O.: Practical object-oriented back-in-time debugging. In: Vitek, J. (ed.) ECOOP 2008. LNCS, vol. 5142, pp. 592–615. Springer, Heidelberg (2008). https://doi.org/10.1007/978-3-540-70592-5_25
23. Marlow, S.: Haskell 2010 Language Report (2010)
24. Milner, R., Tofte, M., MacQueen, D.: The Definition of Standard ML. MIT Press, Cambridge (1997)
25. Moggi, E.: Notions of computation and monads. Inf. Comput. **93**(1), 55–92 (1991). https://doi.org/10.1016/0890-5401(91)90052-4
26. Mosses, P.D.: Modular structural operational semantics. J. Logic Algebraic Program. **60–61**, 195–228 (2004)
27. Mosses, P.D.: Software meta-language engineering and CBS. J. Comput. Lang. **50**, 39–48 (2019). https://doi.org/10.1016/j.jvlc.2018.11.003
28. Mosses, P.D., New, M.J.: Implicit propagation in structural operational semantics. Electron. Notes Theoretical Comput. Sci. **229**(4), 49–66 (2009)
29. Oliveira, B.C.S., Cook, W.R.: Extensibility for the masses. In: Noble, J. (ed.) ECOOP 2012. LNCS, vol. 7313, pp. 2–27. Springer, Heidelberg (2012). https://doi.org/10.1007/978-3-642-31057-7_2
30. Peyton Jones, S. (ed.): Haskell 98, Language and Libraries. The Revised Report. Cambridge University Press (2003)

31. Pickering, M., Wu, N., Kiss, C.: Multi-stage programs in context. In: Eisenberg, R.A. (ed.) Proceedings of the 12th ACM SIGPLAN International Symposium on Haskell, Haskell@ICFP 2019, Berlin, Germany, pp. 71–84. ACM (2019). https://doi.org/10.1145/3331545.3342597

32. Pimentel, J.F., Murta, L., Braganholo, V., Freire, J.: A large-scale study about quality and reproducibility of Jupyter notebooks. In: 2019 IEEE/ACM 16th International Conference on Mining Software Repositories (MSR), pp. 507–517 (2019)

33. Plotkin, G., Pretnar, M.: Handlers of algebraic effects. In: Castagna, G. (ed.) ESOP 2009. LNCS, vol. 5502, pp. 80–94. Springer, Heidelberg (2009). https://doi.org/10.1007/978-3-642-00590-9_7

34. Plotkin, G.D.: A structural approach to operational semantics. J. Logic Algebraic Program. **60–61**, 17–139 (2004)

35. Pothier, G., Tanter, É., Piquer, J.: Scalable omniscient debugging. ACM SIGPLAN Notices **42**(10), 535–552 (2007). https://doi.org/10.1145/1297105.1297067

36. Rein, P., Ramson, S., Lincke, J., Hirschfeld, R., Pape, T.: Exploratory and live, programming and coding. Art Sci. Eng. Program. **3**(1), 1–32 (2018). https://doi.org/10.22152/programming-journal.org/2019/3/1

37. Reynolds, J.C.: Definitional interpreters for higher-order programming languages. In: Proceedings of the ACM Annual Conference, vol. 2, pp. 717–740 (1972)

38. Reynolds, J.C.: Definitional interpreters for higher-order programming languages. High. Order Symbol. Comput. **11**(4), 363–397 (1998)

39. Reynolds, J.C.: Definitional interpreters revisited. High. Order and Symbol. Comput. **11**(4), 355–361 (1998)

40. Rouvoet, A., Bach Poulsen, C., Krebbers, R., Visser, E.: Intrinsically-typed definitional interpreters for linear, session-typed languages. In: Proceedings of the 9th ACM SIGPLAN International Conference on Certified Programs and Proofs (CPP 2020), pp. 284–298 (2020). https://doi.org/10.1145/3372885.3373818

41. Rule, A., Tabard, A., Hollan, J.D.: Exploration and explanation in computational notebooks. In: Proceedings of the 2018 CHI Conference on Human Factors in Computing Systems. CHI 2018, pp. 1–12. ACM (2018)

42. Sewell, P., et al.: Ott: effective tool support for the working semanticist. J. Func. Program. **20**(1), 71–122 (2010). https://doi.org/10.1017/S0956796809990293

43. Swierstra, S.D., Azero Alcocer, P.R., Saraiva, J.: Designing and implementing combinator languages. In: Swierstra, S.D., Oliveira, J.N., Henriques, P.R. (eds.) AFP 1998. LNCS, vol. 1608, pp. 150–206. Springer, Heidelberg (1999). https://doi.org/10.1007/10704973_4

44. Swierstra, W.: Data types à la carte. J. Func. Program. **18**(4), 423–436 (2008). https://doi.org/10.1017/S0956796808006758

45. Trenouth, J.: A survey of exploratory software development. Comput. J. **34**(2), 153–163 (1991). https://doi.org/10.1093/comjnl/34.2.153

46. Van Wyk, E., de Moor, O., Backhouse, K., Kwiatkowski, P.: Forwarding in attribute grammars for modular language design. In: Horspool, R.N. (ed.) CC 2002. LNCS, vol. 2304, pp. 128–142. Springer, Heidelberg (2002). https://doi.org/10.1007/3-540-45937-5_11

47. Vergu, V.A., Neron, P., Visser, E.: DynSem: a DSL for dynamic semantics specification. In: 26th International Conference on Rewriting Techniques and Applications, RTA 2015. Leibniz International Proceedings in Informatics, vol. 36, pp. 365–378. Schloss Dagstuhl - Leibniz-Zentrum für Informatik (2015)

48. Walicki, M., Meldal, S.: Algebraic approaches to nondeterminism - an overview. ACM Comput. Surv. **29**(1), 30–81 (1997)

49. Wu, N., Schrijvers, T., Hinze, R.: Effect handlers in scope. In: Proceedings of the 2014 ACM SIGPLAN Symposium on Haskell. Haskell 2014, pp. 1–12. ACM (2014)

Dynamic Editors for Well-Typed Expressions

Pieter Koopman[1]([envelope]), Steffen Michels[2], and Rinus Plasmeijer[1,2]

[1] Radboud University, Nijmegen, The Netherlands
{pieter,rinus}@cs.ru.nl
[2] TOP Software Solutions, Nijmegen, The Netherlands
steffen@top-software.nl
http://www.ru.nl/icis
http://www.top-software.com

Abstract. Interactive systems may require complex inputs. Domain experts prefer guidance in the construction of these inputs. An ideal system prevents errors and is flexible in the construction and changes of its input. The iTask system generates web-editors given any first-order algebraic data types. The generated web-editors are useful but have their limitations. It is not possible to combine type safety with overloaded operators and preventing unbounded or ill-typed identifiers is impossible. Using phantom types, generalized algebraic datatypes or functions solves the language problems, but they cannot be handled by the datatype generic system. Moreover, changing expressions can require re-entering large parts of the input. We present dynamic editors that can solve all those problems. The programmer specifies the elements of such an editor by functions. The system shows the applicable edit elements in a drop-down menu to the user. The dynamic editor is used recursively to create the arguments for the selected function. Dynamic editors are seamlessly integrated with the ordinary web-editors of the iTask system. The obtained editors guide the users to make correct and type-safe inputs. These editors can be very flexible as well without making strange abstract syntax trees.

Keywords: Dynamics · Web-editor · DSL · Type-safe · Low-code · Task-oriented programming

1 Introduction

Many programs require quite complex inputs from their users. Examples are medical professionals selecting patients, traders inventorying their stock or customers, the coastguard monitoring ships with their distance to each other as well as to ports and wind-parks, teachers selecting students that need additional

Research Paper.

V. Zsók and J. Hughes (Eds.): TFP 2021, LNCS 12834, pp. 44–66, 2021.
https://doi.org/10.1007/978-3-030-83978-9_3

attention and so on. We use a query language about ships as a running example in this paper, but the approach is in no way limited to this application.

Many of these problems are commonly handled in a spreadsheet that contains the data as well as the manipulations of these data. The newest versions of Excel allow user-defined functions to make this easier [6]. This approach is limited to data that are at least stable during processing since the information is stored in a table. For reoccurring types of inputs it is worthwhile to define a Domain Specific Language, DSL, to structure the input. Such a DSL contains the primitives and structures to model the inputs of such a program. This can also work for rapidly changing data.

Programmers often prefer a text-based editor to construct inputs in the DSL, perhaps with some tool support. Many domain experts prefer structure editors that guides them in entering correct expressions in the input DSL. Such a system shows the appropriate constructs at each point of the expression during editing and tries to prevent errors. In this paper we discuss general tooling to implement these structured editors and show how it can be used effectively.

Our DSL editors are part of the iTask system for Task-Oriented Programming, TOP [2,14]. As the name suggests TOP is centred around tasks. Tasks are the units of work in a TOP program. They are created from small basic tasks, like web-editors, and combinators to compose tasks. These tasks can be completely machine-based, but many task mimic interaction with humans. The declarative iTask system generates web-based graphical user-interfaces guiding the interaction. Such a GUI can provide information to the user and can get input from the user to continue the rest of the task. User input varies from pressing a simple button to entering web-forms or the guided constructing of some datastructure. In contrast to ordinary functions, task combinators can be used to observe intermediate states of tasks and act upon the observed state. The iTask system is embedded in the pure functional programming language Clean [15]. Achten wrote a quick introduction for Haskell programmers [3].

In this paper we focus on the design of web-editors to enter inputs that are part of some DSL. Other parts of the iTask system are hardly used and only discussed as far as needed to understand this paper. Our first approach is to define algebraic datatypes to represent the syntax of the input language. Section 2 reviews the possibilities of the existing web-editors to make correct expressions in the input language. This approach is based on generic programming; the web-editors for the datatypes are derived by the compiler. This automatic generation of web-editors is wonderful but comes at a price. The type system ensures type correctness at the level of the host language but not necessarily at the DSL level. Moreover, there is no check on the type nor on the proper definition of identifiers in the DSL.

Section 3 introduces dynamic editors. The drop-down menu is defined by a list of tagged functions. Function types are more expressive than the algebraic data types and can ensure type correctness in the DSL. Only the function producing elements of the desired type are displayed to the user to ensures type correctness of the result. The editor is used recursively to create the arguments of the chosen function. Well-typed identifiers in the DSL are obtained by selecting them from a list of typed identifiers. This is discussed in Sect. 4.

Section 2 introduces the running example of this paper and the limitations of the generic derivation of web-editors. In Sect. 5 we show how one can make a type safe editor for the datatypes used in Sect. 2 using dynamic editors and type tags. Using GADTs of shallow embedding ensures the type correctness during the entire lifespan of the editor results. This is shown in Sects. 6 and 7 for our running example. Finally, we discuss related work and draw conclusions in Sect. 9.

The main contributions of this paper are:

- the introduction of dynamic editors. These structured web-editors are used to create DSL-expressions interactively while enforcing type-constraints on the fly. This can be used for types where the generic algorithm cannot be used to derive such editors;
- we demonstrate how to ensure that all variables are well-typed by selecting them from a identifier store;
- we show how the dynamic editors can be prepared for flexible changes of the input.
- we demonstrate how dynamic editors can generate type-safe ADTs;
- we show that dynamic web-editors can handle GADTs;
- we show how to create type-safe editors for shallow embedded DSLs.

The dynamic editor library used in this paper is part of the standard iTask system available at clean.cs.ru.nl/iTasks. The examples in this paper can be found at gitlab.science.ru.nl/pieter/tfp-2021-dynamic-editors.

2 Algebraic Data Types for Queries

The running example of this paper is based on a real-world application of the iTask system. The users of this system write queries over ships, ports and wind-parks as well as their distance in some part of the sea. The real application also includes owners of these ships, their history and destinations. We omit these aspects since they would make our example over complicated.

The current position and data of all ships are provided by the Automatic Identification System, AIS. All ships are broadcast their name, size, position, voyage date and other relevant information frequently. The required frequency is mainly dependent on the speed of the vessel. Everyone can receive this data and use it. Based on the received data websites like vesselfinder.com and marinetraffic.com show world wide real-time vessel positions. There are several sources of AIS data available that includes data of vessels that our outside broadcast range. We use simplified and static data in this paper to mimic this data stream as simple as possible.

The data of ships, ports and wind-parks are each stored in a tailor-made record. We use a list of these records as the test data in our programs. Our example DSL is a query language over ships, ports and wind-parks. The language contains the type Gen to mimic generation. It introduces ship, port or wind-park identifier, conditions to select objects and there is a single return expression determining the result. The nature of expressions is similar to list-comprehensions. The datastructure correspond one to one with the grammar of our DSL. Boolean expressions have their own datatype Cond. This ensures the condition always represents a Boolean result. A less pleasant consequence is that the overloaded equality Eq cannot be applied to Boolean arguments.

A complete DSL will contain more comparison and arithmetic operations. We have reduced it to the bare minimum needed to illustrate the architecture of the example.

```
:: Gen
    = Ship Name Gen | Park Name Gen | Port Name Gen
    | Cond Cond Gen | Ret  Expr
:: Cond
    = LE Expr Expr | Eq Expr Expr | Not Cond | And Cond Cond
    | Flag Expr [Country] | Name Expr [String] | Kind Expr [Kind]
:: Expr
    = Var Name | Num Real | Name Expr | Add Expr Expr
    | Distance Expr Expr | Gen Gen
:: Kind    = Navy | Fisher | Tanker | Cargo | Tugboat
:: Country = NL | UK | DE | FR | BE | BR | VE | PH | DK | LR | MT
:: Name    :== String
```

A simple example is a query that yields the name of all ships with a flag from the Netherlands or the United Kingdom.

```
e :: Gen
e = Ship s (Cond (Flag (Var s) [NL,UK]) (Ret (Name (Var s))))

s :: Name
s = "s"
```

The reason we have chosen the iTask system as host for our web-editors for DSLs is that it can derive those editors for algebraic datatypes. This is done by type generic programming [1,4,8]. The idea is that Clean knows how to transform between a datatype and its generic representation. This type generic representation is built with a small number of primitives like the choice, EITHER, and the sum, PAIR, of elements. The iTask system knows how to make editors for the generic primitives and hence the generic representation of our tailor-made datatypes for the DSL. All we need to do is deriving the generic instances by:

derive class iTask Gen, Cond, Expr, Country, Status, Res

2.1   Editors for ADT-Based Queries

Now we can use editors for these types in the iTask system. The user gets a drop-down menu to select a constructor of the desired type. After this selection, there appear editors for the arguments of the constructor. Edit boxes are used for integers and strings. Figure 1 shows two snapshots of the generated editors. The left-hand side is an editor for queries and the associated result. Such a result is automatically computed by the iTask system as soon as the editor represents a well-typed value. The right-hand side shows the drop-down menu for type Gen. Using tuning combinators, like ≪@, and cascading style sheets the layout of the editor can be improved.

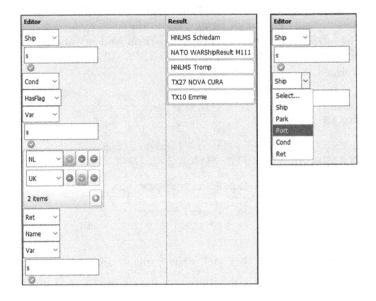

Fig. 1. Screenshots of the DSL editor.

The entire code needed to generate the task-based web interface for the editor and evaluator display on the left in Fig. 1 requires a start rule to evaluate the genTask. The programmer can use cascading style sheets to improve the appearance of the program.

```
Start world = doTasks genTask world
```

```
genTask :: Task Gen
genTask =
  withShared e λsds.
    (Title "Editor" @≫ updateSharedInformation [] sds) -||-
    (Title "Result" @≫ viewSharedInformation [ViewAs run] sds) ≪@ ArrangeHorizontal
```

The function withShared makes a shared data source sds for of type Gen with initial value e as defined above. The updateSharedInformation tasks is a generated editor for this sds. The second task displays the value of this sds after applying the function run that evaluates the expression. The task combinator -||- composes these tasks in parallel. The nature of shared data stores updates the value displayed as soon as the editor contains a new valid expression.

The expression Expr represents values of type Ship, Port, Park, Real and String. Defining a separate type for each of these types makes the language much larger and enforces us to have many variants of overloaded operations like Eq and Distance.

A single type representing these different evaluation results is needed in our strongly typed host language. The type Res does just that, it adds an appropriate constructor to distinguish the various types.

```
:: Res = ShipResult Ship | PortResult Port | ParkResult Park
       | RealResult Real | BoolResult Bool | StringResult String
```

For the evaluation of expressions we define an environment Env that ties names to Res values. The implementation of this environment is unimportant and omitted. The tie adds a new binding and read yields the value associated with that name or an error message. In Haskell the type will be written as Name → Res → Env → Env.

```
:: Eval a = Eval (Env → MaybeError String [a])
:: Env

new  :: Env
tie  :: Name Res Env → Env
read :: Name → Eval Res
```

We define the class eval for the evaluation of the types in our DSL and instances of the monadic classes for Eval. The instances of this class are straightforward. We only list the instance for Expr to show that we still need quite some runtime type checking and error handling despite the strong typing of the host language.

```
class eval a :: a → Eval Res

instance eval Expr where
  eval expr = case expr of
    Var name = read name
    Num real = pure (RealResult real)
    Distance x y = eval x >>=λa. eval y >>=λb.pure (RealResult (distance a b))
    Add x y = eval x >>=λa. eval y >>=λb.case (a, b) of
                    (RealResult v, RealResult w) = pure (RealResult (v + w))
                    _ = fail "Add needs two real arguments"
    Name e = eval e >>=λa.case a of
                    ShipResult s = pure (StringResult s.Ship.name)
                    PortResult s = pure (StringResult s.Port.name)
                    ParkResult s = pure (StringResult s.Park.name)
                    _ = fail "Name: this has no name"
    Gen g = eval g
```

2.2 Evaluation of the ADT Approach

This Section shows that the iTask system is very suited to make editors for an ADT based input language. We just have to define the appropriate datatypes and the generic machinery for the iTask system derives the required machinery. However, the ADT has approach also has several significant drawbacks.

– The type expression allows instances that are correct in the host language but must be considered as a type error in our DSL. For instance, we can check if

42.0 is less than some ship s, compute the distance between a number and a name, and so one.

- We can introduce specific types for types of sub-expressions, like Cond for Boolean expressions. Our simple example shows that this limits overloading, there is no equality for Boolean expressions. When we would introduce special types for all type in the DSL we would need N equalities for a language with N types and even $O(N^2)$ variants of the distance operator. This does not scale to serious examples.
- There is no check on the identifiers in the DSL. Any string represents an identifier of an arbitrary type. The host language cannot check if the identifier is properly defined nor if it as the correct type. Here the allowed types for identifiers are Ship, Port and Park.

We can define a type checker for DSL expression but that will only run at the same time as the evaluator. After the user has defined a complete DSL expression the system can indicate that it contains an error. We highly prefer a system that prevents errors while an expression is constructed over a version that indicates the mistakes afterwards. Fortunately, several approaches are well known in the functional DSL community. For instance, we can add type information, use GADTs or use function types in a shallow embedding. All of these techniques have in common that it requires features that cannot be handled by the generic system. Hence, we cannot derive iTask based web-editors for these approaches. Typical examples of constructs that prevent generic derivation are phantom types, extensionally quantified variables, class constraints and functions [10]. We introduce dynamic editors as a solution. They can be used to make type-safe editors for all listed methods to create type-safe DSLs.

3   Dynamic Editors

The generic generation of web-editors for datatypes is quite nice. However, it cannot yield the amount of control we need in our DSL representing a somewhat complex input language. The expressions are well-typed instances of the ADT, but the DSL is often more strict. In this section, we introduce a concise declarative way to specify editors that do yield the amount of control required. The dynamic editor will display a drop-down menu. The items in this menu are specified by labelled functions. The label specifies the name displayed as well as the tag used in the internal representation. The function specifies the production rule for this edit clause. The editor is used recursively to generate the arguments for the function in the chosen edit element. Although all edit options are specified in a single list, the dynamic editor will display only those options that produce a type that fits the required type in the given context.

We will explain this in more detail using a simple example. It contains integer values and Peano numbers defined as :: Num = Zero | Succ Num. The operations for Num are implemented in the well-known way. Our editors have addition and equality of both types of numbers as edit clauses.

A dynamic editor is a list of groups. The name of the group is displayed as a separator in the drop-down menu show dynamically. Each group consists of dynamic editor elements de, or constant editor elements ce[1]

```
exprEditor :: DynamicEditor a | TC a
exprEditor = DynamicEditor
  [ DynamicConsGroup "Functions"
    [ de "+ Int"   (dynamic (+)  :: Int Int → Int)
    , de "- Int"   (dynamic (-)  :: Int Int → Int)
    , de "== Int"  (dynamic (==) :: Int Int → Bool)
    ]
  , DynamicConsGroup "Peano"
    [ de "Succ"    (dynamic Succ)
    , de "Zero"    (dynamic Zero)
    , de "+ Num"   (dynamic (+)  :: Num Num → Num)
    , de "== Num"  (dynamic (==) :: Num Num → Bool)
    , de "mixed"   (dynamic \n i→toInt n == i :: Num Int → Bool)
    ]
  , DynamicConsGroup "Basic Editors"
    [ ce "Int value" intEditor
    , ce "Bool value" boolEditor
    ]
  ]
```

To make such an editor definition well-typed we have to pack the functions specifying the edit clauses in a **dynamic** [13]. These dynamics are all of type Dynamic. A program can check the type stored in a dynamic by a pattern match. If the actual value of the Dynamic matches the specified type, we can extract its value. This ensures that a program using dynamics is statically still well-typed.

This is illustrated by the function match. It checks whether the given dynamic has a type that matches the type a of the given argument. The class constraint TC a guarantees that elements of type a can be stored and retrieved from a dynamic. Alternative one checks if the type is equal to the given type. The caret symbol ^ is used as the suffix of a type pattern variable a in a dynamic pattern match to indicate that an overloaded type variable is used, instead of a type pattern variable of the dynamic. The next line matches any function in the dynamic. If there is such a function f, we give it an argument undef and call match recursively. In this way, we can handle functions with an arbitrary number of arguments. The dynamic does not match in all other situations. Dynamic editors use such an algorithm to determine which alternatives should be displayed.

---

[1] Actually these elements are abbreviations of slightly more general items in the library. The items in the library allow different tags and names displayed. This can be convenient, but it is more verbose and we do not need this additional flexibility here.

```
de name dyn = functionConsDyn name name dyn
ce name edt = customEditorCons name name edt
```

```
match :: a Dynamic → Bool | TC a
match _ (x::a^) = True
match a (f::b→c) = match a (dynamic f undef)
match _ _ = False
```

The type of exprEditor shows that this editor can yield values of any type a. The context determines the resulting type. We assume that the context requires Bool in our example. This implies that only the alternatives labelled == Int, == Num, mixed and Bool value match the required type. Only those alternatives will be displayed to the user. Suppose that our user selects the alternative mixed. This needs two arguments; the first has type Num and the second type Int. These arguments can be constructed in an arbitrary order. Our editor is used recursively for those arguments and again displays only the alternatives matching the required type. Figure 2 shows some screenshots of this editor in action[2]. The pictures show that the editor displays only the applicable alternatives in each situation. This keeps the drop-down menu as short as possible and ensures that the user cannot construct ill-typed values.

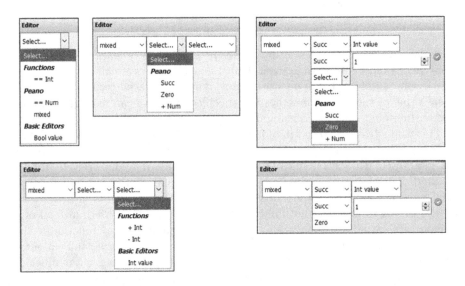

Fig. 2. Screenshots of our first dynamic editor. The appearance can be improved by style sheets.

The basic editors defined in the last group of this example are the generic editors for integers and Booleans. They use the basic generic editor gEditor.

---

[2] We used some CCS annotations to obtain horizontal layout and grey boxes to group elements. Since we focus on correctness we do not discuss this fine-tuning of editors in this paper. We show the default layout offered by the system and do not spent any effort in beautifying its appearance. For real-world application polishing the interface is important.

```
intEditor :: Editor Int (?Int)
intEditor = gEditor{|*|} EditValue

boolEditor :: Editor Bool (?Bool)
boolEditor = gEditor{|*|} EditValue
```

When we derive the class iTask for Num we can also make such an editor for this type. This can replace the dynamic editor alternatives labelled Succ and Zero in the editor above or they can be used in combination.

3.1   Using Dynamic Editors

Dynamic editors can be used like other editors in the iTask system. In the edit options of the editor we just have to indicate that we want our newly defined dynamic editor instead of the generic version. The function editor show how our last dynamic editor is used in an edit task.

```
editor :: Task (DynamicEditorValue (Expr a)) | iTask a
editor = enterInformation [EnterUsing id (dynamicEditor exprEditor)]
```

In the same way, we can define tasks to update a given value and to update information stored in a shared data source.

The example above shows that dynamic editors can handle datatypes, like Num, as well as operators, like + and ==, and other functions, like mixed. These functions and operators are not immediately reduced but handled like constructors in a datatype. This allows the user to observe and change the expression before it is evaluated. The dynamic editor produces a DynamicEditorValue a. This is a Rose tree like structure where the tags of the dynamic edit elements are stored. Ordinary iTask editors are JSON encoded in this tree, this encoding is also used in the ordinary iTask editors.

The implementation of dynamic editors creates a drop-down menu with the matching edit alternatives using the low-level iTask web-primitives. This ensures that the dynamic editor has the same look and feel as the rest of the iTask system. Just like the rest of the iTask system its appearance can be tuned by custom made cascading style sheets, see www.w3.org/Style/CSS/Overview.en. html.

3.2   Using the Value of a Dynamic Editor

The function valueOf transforms a DynamicEditorValue a to a maybe value a given the editor and the tree. This is done by applying the functions indicated by the tags of the dynamic editor. It will only return nothing if the current editor value is Undefined.

```
valueOf :: (DynamicEditor a) (DynamicEditorValue a) → ?a | TC a
```

The selection of functions based on the tags in the DynamicEditorValue explains why these tags must be unique. The editor checks the uniqueness of the tags in the editor.

3.3   Overloading in Dynamic Editors

In the editor above we use two instances of the equality operator == in similar dynamic edit clauses. One for type Int and one for Num.

```
, de "== Int" (dynamic (==) :: Int Int → Bool)
, de "== Num" (dynamic (==) :: Num Num → Bool)
```

It might look attractive to replace those clauses with a single overloaded version.

```
, de "== dyn" (dynamic (==) :: ∀ t: t t → Bool | == t)
```

This formulation is accepted by the compiler, but it is not as pleasant as it looks. The overloading of the equality operator cannot be solved in this situation. This implies that the compiler adds an additional runtime argument to this equality function. This dictionary will contain at runtime the correct equality for the actual type. The dynamic system will see this dictionary as an additional argument of the == dyn editor and generate an edit field for it. Since these dictionaries are not first-class language elements, it is not possible to make the required dynamic editor alternatives.

A workaround is to define the required equality manually and apply it explicitly. We store the comparison operators in a datatype :: Comp t = Comp (t t→Bool)[3]. Appropriate dynamic edit alternatives are:

```
, de "== cmp" (dynamic λ (Comp f) .f :: ∀ t: (Comp t) t t → Bool)
, de "Eq Int" (dynamic Comp (==) :: Comp Int)
, de "LE Int" (dynamic Comp (<)  :: Comp Int)
, de "Eq Num" (dynamic Comp (==) :: Comp Num)
```

Note that we do not need a class constraint here.

This works correctly but has unpleasant behaviour. Argument two and three of the == cmp have type t. This implies that any alternative of the editor will be available, for serious editors this will be a long list of options. Only when values are supplied for at least two of the arguments the dynamic editor can do the unification to check that the types t are equal. The dynamic editor will indicate a unification error, but this can only be done after the error has been made. We want to prevent the possibility to make type errors and show only the appropriate edit options to the user. Hence, we highly prefer the monomorphic edit options == Int and == Num.

The higher-order compare function can be very useful to make the editor more flexible. Assume that we have also a less than operator for integers in our system. We can define this in the same style as the == Int. when the user-created large arguments for the equality operator and changes her mind she will replace the == Int with < Int and has to create the arguments again.

We can allow the change of comparator by defining an editor alternative Comp Int.

```
, de "Comp Int" (dynamic λ (Comp f) .f :: (Comp Int) Int Int → Bool)
```

---

[3] Without such a datatype the dynamic editor will go into the recursion to make editors for the arguments of the comparison function.

All arguments have monomorphic types. Hence, no class constraints are needed and the dynamic editor shows only the correct options to the user. However, when the user wants to change the operator, this can be done without touching the arguments. We have gained flexibility in the use of the editor. It is easy to see that a similar approach can be used for binary operators like addition, subtraction and multiplication.

3.4   Extendable Expressions

The inputs provided by the domain experts will vary over time. Typically there is some trial and error in the creation of these inputs. The operator of our ships query program formulates a query and looks at the result. Based on these observations the query is fine-tuned by the user to improve the results. It is convenient when the user can reuse as much as possible of the existing query to update it to the new one. By storing the input in a shared data source the user can simultaneously edit the input and observe the result like we did in our first edit task in Sect. 2.

The selectable comparison operators introduced above make expressions more flexible. The design of operations like Flag also contribute to the flexibility of inputs. It is always easy to add or remove a few elements to the list of countries used in these conditions. Nevertheless, users of DSL-editors created with our dynamic editors report that they have to recreate sub-expressions too often because they have forgotten some detail. Examples are adding a small constant, multiplying a number by 2, or adding a condition like the kind of vessel. This is just a new instance a well-known problem in structured editors; these editors help users to create correct expressions. The price to be paid is that it is not possible to update nodes in the tree while preserving the existing sub-expressions.

With the addition of a datatype, we can make editors that can handle these kinds of changes while the sub-expressions constructed so far are untouched. To illustrate this approach we make a very simple expression type[4].

:: Expr a = ∃ b: Binop (b→b→a) (Expr b) (Expr b) | Lit a

We use the type BinOp in the editor to hold the operations in this language. It is a small generalisation of the type Comp used above. The constructor is needed again to prevent that the dynamic editor starts creating arguments for this function.

:: BinOp a b = BinOp (a→a→b)

For the extensions, we define a datatype Ext. It contains the operator to apply and its right-hand argument as parameters. The type synonym BinOpExt is a convenient abbreviation for the type that needs an operator, two arguments and a list of extensions. The function binop folds such a BinOpExt to a regular expression.

---

[4] For pretty-printing of the expressions it might be necessary to add the name of the operation. We omit it to keep the example as small as possible.

```
:: Ext b = Ext (BinOp b b) (Expr b)
:: BinOpExt a b:== (BinOp a b) (Expr a) (Expr a) [Ext b] → Expr b

binOp :: (BinOp a b) (Expr a) (Expr a) [Ext b] → Expr b
binOp (BinOp f) a b l = foldr (λ (Ext (BinOp g) c) d.Oper g d c) (Oper f a b) l
```

Note that the expression type is not changed to incorporate these extensions. We can of course add them to the type Expr, but there is no need. We prefer to keep the expressions simple and just add these feature to the dynamic editor.

Using these tools we can define an extendable dynamic editor. The group Functions contains generators for the various binary operations in our expressions. Like above we have made separate clauses for the various types. The group Operations contains the operations in our language. They are used in binary operations as well as in their extensions. The group Lists contains the editors for the various expressions. Finally, there are editors specified for the literals in our expressions.

```
exprEditor2 :: DynamicEditor (Expr t) | TC t
exprEditor2 = DynamicEditor
  [ DynamicConsGroup "Functions"
    [ de "Logic"       (dynamic binOp :: BinOpExt Bool Bool)
    , de "Arith"       (dynamic binOp :: BinOpExt Real Real)
    , de "Comparison"  (dynamic binOp :: BinOpExt Real Bool)
    , de "Ext"         (dynamic Ext   :: ∀ b: (BinOp b b) (Expr b) → Ext b)
    ]
  , DynamicConsGroup "Operations"   // Add other operations by need
    [ de "add"       (dynamic BinOp (+)  :: BinOp Real Real)  «@ UseAsDefault
    , de "multiply"  (dynamic BinOp (*)  :: BinOp Real Real)
    , de "smaller"   (dynamic BinOp (<)  :: BinOp Real Bool)  «@ UseAsDefault
    , de "equal real" (dynamic BinOp (==) :: BinOp Real Bool)
    , de "equal bool" (dynamic BinOp (==) :: BinOp Bool Bool)
    , de "and"       (dynamic BinOp (&&) :: BinOp Bool Bool)  «@ UseAsDefault
    , de "or"        (dynamic BinOp (||) :: BinOp Bool Bool)
    ]
  , DynamicConsGroup "Lists"         // to make lists of extensions
    [ lc "Ext bool" idExtBool «@ HideIfOnlyChoice
    , lc "Ext real" idExtReal «@ HideIfOnlyChoice
    ]
  , DynamicConsGroup "Basic Editors"
    [ ce "Real value"  realLitEditor
    , ce "Bool value"  boolLitEditor
    ]
  ]
```

Figure 3 shows snapshots of this editor is use. The topmost editor contains the expressions 7 + 14 == 42 without any extensions. The circles labelled + are the placeholders for the list of extensions. At the bottom an extension is added to become (7 + 14) * 2 == 42. It is of course possible to make the expression 7 + (14 * 2) == 42. This does not require extensions, just replace the real value 14 with the appropriate multiplication. Here we do not add extensions to literals, but this can be done similarly.

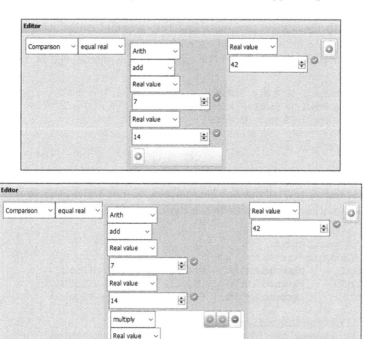

Fig. 3. The extendable dynamic editor in use. At the bottom we have added ⋆ 2

4   Properly Defined DSL Identifiers

In the previous section, we showed how to make web-editors in iTask that cannot
be derived by the generic system. The remaining problem to make only correct
DSL expressions identified in Sect. 2 is properly defined identifiers. When we
define variables by a construct like Var String, they can have any type and every
string serves as an identifier name. We can solve both problems by selecting
typed identifiers from a given collection instead of using arbitrary strings as a
name.

Such a collection can be defined by a State. This is a list of bindings. Each
binding is a record with a name idnt and a value. To represent identifiers of
different types in the state we have to store these values as a Dynamic.

```
:: Bind a = {idnt :: String, val :: a}
:: State:== [Bind Dynamic]
```

All we have to do next is parametrizing the dynamic editor with the current state and generate an edit element for each binding in the state. The type E is a very simple GADT with explicit type conversions as introduced by Hinze [5][5]

```
:: E a
  = Add (BM a Real) (E Real) (E Real)
  | And (BM a Bool) (E Bool) (E Bool)
  | Eq  (BM a Bool) (E Real) (E Real)
  | Lit a
  | Var String
```

```
:: BM a b = {ab :: a → b, ba :: b → a}
```

Since the bimap record BM contains functions we cannot derive generic web-editors for it. The function exprEditor defines a dynamic editor for it.

```
exprEditor :: DynamicEditor (E t)
exprEditor = DynamicEditor
  [ DynamicConsGroup "Operators"
    [ de "Add"     (dynamic Add bm :: (E Real) (E Real) → E Real)
    , de "And"     (dynamic And bm :: (E Bool) (E Bool) → E Bool)
    , de "Eq"      (dynamic Eq  bm :: (E Real) (E Real) → E Bool)
    ]
  , DynamicConsGroup "Identifiers"
    [ de idnt (dynamic (Var idnt) :: E t) \\ {idnt,val=x::t} ← state]
  , DynamicConsGroup "Basic Editors"
    [ ce "Real value"  realLitEditor
    , ce "Bool value"  boolLitEditor
    ]
  ]
```

The important point here is that we do not add a clause that turns variable names into identifiers in our expression of type E a. The group Identifiers generates the identifiers from the state. We can use this editor just like the previous dynamic editors. Here this state is fixed, but using a parametrisedDynamicEditor we can also take this function from a dynamically changing shared data source. Our dynamic editor should have type State → DynamicEditor (E t).

Note that we have to specify types for Add, And and Eq. The Clean compiler is not able to derive those types.

The previous section shows how to define web-editors that cannot be derived by the generic system. This section reveals how we can guarantee that only properly typed and existing identifiers are used. The combination of these techniques can create type-safe editors for our DSLs. In the next sections, we show how we can use dynamic editors to make type-safe web-editors for ship queries in various representations of the DSL.

---

[5] If Clean would have a GADT extension like Haskell this type could be specified as:

```
:: E a
  = Add :: (E Real) (E Real) → E Real
  | And :: (E Bool) (E Bool) → E Bool
  | Eq  :: (E Real) (E Real) → E Bool
  | Lit :: a → E a
  | Var :: String → E a
```

5   Ensuring Type Safety by Phantom Types

The simplest approach to make a type-safe version of our DSL is to reuse the same simple DSL form Sect. 2. Only during editing, we use additional type tags to indicate the type we think that the expression should represent. For this purpose, we define a general type Tagged a b. Here a is the actual type, in our application Expr, and b is the type that should be stored in that expression. Since the phantom type b distinguishes Boolean expressions from other expressions there is no need for separate types Cond and Expr. By unifying those types the problem that we cannot represent equality for Boolean expressions disappears[6].

```
:: Tagged a b =: Tagged a

:: Gen
    = Ship Name Gen | WindPark Name Gen | Port Name Gen
    | Cond Expr Gen | Ret Expr
:: Expr
    = Eq Expr Expr | And Expr Expr | Add Expr Expr
    | Flag Expr [Country] | Var Name | Real Real
    | Distance Expr Expr | Position Expr
```

The make the definition of the dynamic editor more concise we introduce some helper functions to handle the tags and a type abbreviation.

```
T  f (Tagged x)             = Tagged (f x)
Tx f (Tagged x) y           = Tagged (f x y)
TT f (Tagged x) (Tagged y) = Tagged (f x y)
```

```
:: TExpr a :== Tagged Expr a
```

With these tools, the dynamic editor for tagged expressions is quite concise[7]. We typically need a single line for each alternative. Just as in Sect. 4 we obtain the names of objects from a state. The group Names generate these names as tagged strings. The group Identifiers make the tagged expressions with names for the state. The generators themselves obtain no tags since we allow any type there. The group Know Ports generates the position of all ports known as a convenient shortcut for the user. Without this shortcut, the user needs to introduce a port variable and adds a condition that limits the name of the port to the desired port. The group Expressions contains some interesting expression elements, the full list is too long to include here.

```
exprEditor :: State → DynamicEditor Gen
exprEditor state = DynamicEditor
  [DynamicConsGroup "Generators"
    [de "Ship"   (dynamic λ (Tagged name) .Ship name :: (Tagged String Ship) Gen→sGen)
    ,de "Cond"   (dynamic λ (Tagged expr) .Cond expr :: (TExpr Bool) Gen → Gen)
    ,de "Return" (dynamic λ (Tagged e) .Ret e :: ∀ a: (TExpr a) → Gen)
    ]
```

---

[6] We have dropped operators with similar types to the listed constructors to safe space.

[7] Due to space limitations we list only the interesting clauses here. Alternatives that are very similar to the one listed here are omitted.

```
,DynamicConsGroup "Identifiers"
  [de ("Var " + idnt) (dynamic (Tagged (Var idnt)) :: TExpr t)
  \\ {idnt,val=x::t} ←state]
,DynamicConsGroup "Names"
  [de ("Name " + idnt) (dynamic (Tagged idnt) :: Tagged String t)
  \\ {idnt,val=x::t} ←state]
,DynamicConsGroup "Known Ports"
  [de ("Port "+p.Port.name) (dynamic Tagged (Position (Lit p)) :: TExpr Position)
  \\ p←ports]
,DynamicConsGroup "Expressions"
  [de "Less"      (dynamic TT LE :: (TExpr Real) (TExpr Real) → TExpr Bool)
  ,de "Eq"        (dynamic TT Eq :: ∀ a: (TExpr a) (TExpr a) → TExpr Bool)
  ,de "And"       (dynamic TT And :: (TExpr Bool) (TExpr Bool) → TExpr Bool)
  ,de "Not"       (dynamic T  Not :: (TExpr Bool) → TExpr Bool)
  ,de "Has flag"  (dynamic Tx Flag :: (TExpr Ship) [Country] → TExpr Bool)
  ,de "Number"    (dynamic λx.Tagged (Real x) :: Real → TExpr Real)
  ,de "Distance"  (dynamic TT Distance:: (TExpr Position) (TExpr Position)→TExpr Real)
  ,de "Ship pos"  (dynamic T  Position :: (TExpr Ship) → TExpr Position)
  ,de "Port pos"  (dynamic T  Position :: (TExpr Port) → TExpr Position)
  ,de "Name ship" (dynamic T  Name :: (TExpr Ship) → TExpr String)
  ,de "Name park" (dynamic T  Name :: (TExpr Park) → TExpr String)
  ]
// Editors for basic types are equal to the other editor examples.
```

Note that the alternative for Eq is completely overloaded. Since we have only a fixed number of types in our DSL there is no need for a class constraint. The types of both arguments are unified at runtime. The user can make a type error which will be indicated as soon as it is present. The editor does not yield a result until this error is corrected.

The case for Distance uses the new type Position to avoid a long list of cases that enumerate all possible combinations here. With positions of ships, parks and ports and fixed positions we would need 16 editor alternatives otherwise.

These datatypes in our DSL are very similar to the DSL used in Sect. 2. The evaluator has an identical structure. Based on the datatype alone it has to cope with possible type errors. When we construct instances of the DSL with the editor above, type errors should not occur. The tags ensure that only well-typed instances are created.

The only remaining problem is that the user can select a properly typed identifier that is not introduced by the associated generator in the query. If we assume that using this variable is intentional we can easily fix the problem. We just scan the current expression for variables that occur in the state and do not have the associated generator. It is a simple transformation of the input expression to add the missing generators. The user will soon discover that it is not necessary to write the generators and rely on this automatic introduction of variables from the state.

6   Generalized Algebraic Data Types

Generalized Algebraic Data Types are a way to exploit the provided type-information such that we do not have to pack all results into a single result type [9,18]. We base our GADT representation on the extendable expressions from Sect. 3.4. The only thing we have to add are the types for our ship expressions and special operations like Distance, FlagIn and Kind. The following Expr implements such a GADT. Note that we use a position argument PosArg to limit the number of cases we have to write in de dynamic editor. It can be used for position editors, as well as any object that has a position, e.g. Ship, Port or Park.

```
:: Expr a
   = Not (BM a Bool) (Expr Bool)
   | ∃ b: OneOf (BM a Bool) (b b→Bool) (Expr b) [b]
   | ∃ b: Oper (b b→a) (Expr b) (Expr b)
   | Flag (BM a Country) (Expr Ship)
   | ∃ b: Name (BM a Name) (Expr b) & type, name b
   | Var Name & TC a
   | Lit a & type a
   | Distance (BM a Real) PosArg PosArg
:: PosArg = ∃ a: PosArg (Expr a) & toPosition a
```

We define the interesting cases of the corresponding dynamic editor in the same style. We define a special manipulation function for the single argument operator Not. The same holds for the OneOf expressions to check the flag or kind of a ship.

```
, DynamicConsGroup "Expressions"
  [ de "Not"          (dynamic expOp o Not bm)
  , de "Comp Real"    (dynamic binOp :: BinOpExt Real Bool)
  , de "Comp String"  (dynamic binOp :: BinOpExt String Bool)
  , de "Logic"        (dynamic binOp :: BinOpExt Bool Bool)
  , de "Arith"        (dynamic binOp :: BinOpExt Real Real)
  , de "Flag in"      (dynamic λx y.expOp (OneOf bm (==) x y)
                        :: (Expr Country) [Country] [Ext Bool] → Expr Bool)
  , de "Distance"     (dynamic Distance bm)
  , de "Ship pos"     (dynamic PosArg :: (Expr Ship) → PosArg)
  , de "Port pos"     (dynamic PosArg :: (Expr Port) → PosArg)
  , de "Flag"         (dynamic Flag bm)
  , de "Ext"          (dynamic Ext :: ∀ b: (BinOp b b) (Expr b) → Ext b)
  ]
```

Due to the nature of GADTs, the evaluator knows what the type of all expressions is and does not need a result type to pack all possible results. The type system guarantees that runtime type errors cannot occur. This makes the evaluator much simpler.

However, there are also some small drawbacks to this approach. Since expressions can now take any type a as an argument we need some additional code to ensure that things will be evaluated properly. This is reflected for instance in the fact that we now need a separate compare for reals and one for Booleans. The type PosArg needs a type constraint in order to ensure that we can apply the function toPosition to the arguments. In most situations, these small things are outweighed by the advantages of the GADT.

Since this produces a data type we can apply a similar DSL transformation to add missing generators for ships, ports and wind-parks.

7   Shallow Embedding

A shallow embedded DSL represents the language constructs by functions in the host language. This is efficient since there is no construction of intermediate datatypes. These functions are limited to a single interpretation of the DSL. Language transformations, like the introduction of generators for used variables, are impossible. This makes this representation less suited for our running example. Nevertheless, we show the main part of the implementation to illustrate the possibilities of our dynamic editors.

The DSL directly calls the implementation clauses from the evaluator of the GADT representation in Sect. 6. In its turn, this is a stronger typed version of the evaluator in Sect. 2. Like always, we need some constructors to prevent the dynamic editor from making editors for the arguments of higher-order functions and to distinguish types. The constructor Eval used for the Monadic types in the evaluator prevents the dynamic editing system from generating too much argument editors. We define a type synonym and some convenience functions to make the edit cases one-liners. The interesting part of the dynamic editor for our shallow embedded DSL for ships becomes:

```
:: Gen :== Eval Res
:: VarName a = VarName String

binOp o x y = fmap o x <*> y
newId list (VarName name) e = gen name list e
rturn tag g = g >>= λs.pure $ tag s
cond c gen = c >>= λb. guard b >> | gen
oneOf f e l = e >>= λs.pure (isMember (f s) l)

exprEditor :: State → DynamicEditor Gen
exprEditor state = DynamicEditor
  [ DynamicConsGroup "Generators"
    [ de "Ship"         (dynamic newId ships       :: (VarName Ship) Gen → Gen)
    , de "Port"         (dynamic newId ports       :: (VarName Port) Gen → Gen)
    , de "Return Ship"  (dynamic rturn ShipResult  :: (Eval Ship)   → Gen)
    , de "Return name"  (dynamic rturn StringResult :: (Eval String) → Gen)
    , de "Condition"    (dynamic cond              :: (Eval Bool) Gen → Gen)
    ]
  , DynamicConsGroup "Expressions"
    [ de "Less"         (dynamic binOp (<)  :: (Eval Real) (Eval Real) → Eval Bool)
    , de "Eq real"      (dynamic binOp (==) :: (Eval Real) (Eval Real) → Eval Bool)
    , de "Eq position"  (dynamic binOp (==) :: (Eval Pos) (Eval Pos) → Eval Bool)
    , de "And"          (dynamic binOp (&&) :: (Eval Bool) (Eval Bool) → Eval Bool)
    , de "Not"          (dynamic fmap not   :: (Eval Bool) → Eval Bool)
    , de "Has flag"     (dynamic oneOf (λs.s.flag) :: (Eval Ship) [Flag] → Eval Bool)
    , de "Has kind"     (dynamic oneOf (λs.s.kind) :: (Eval Ship) [Kind] → Eval Bool)
    , de "Distance"     (dynamic binOp distance :: (Eval Pos) (Eval Pos) → Eval Real)
    , de "Position ship" (dynamic fmap toPosition :: (Eval Ship) → Eval Pos)
    , de "Position port" (dynamic fmap toPosition :: (Eval Port) → Eval Pos)
    ]
  // Basic editors and lists similar to previous examples
```

This dynamic editor works just as fine as the previous editors. Whenever desired we can build additional flexibility in the editor like we did before. Since the domain expert has to introduce each quantifier explicitly this version is less convenient for this user. Of course, we can implicitly introduce quantification over every variable in the state, but this has a runtime penalty. If there are S ships in the system and we introduce N unused ship identifiers the execution time will increase by a factor $O(S^N)$.

8 Related Work

There is a plethora of ways to create web-pages is various programming languages these days. See [7] for an up-to-date overview of Haskell based systems. Yesod [19], Happstack [20] and Servant [11] aim to make type-safe web-pages. In those tools one defines web-pages by their elements and associated handlers. With dynamic editors the programmer specifies DSL constructs and the corresponding web-pages are generated. In our opinion this yields a higher level of abstraction and a more declarative and convenient approach for programmers.

The low-code approach aims to develop complete applications interactively [22]. This name was coined by Richardson [16]. Gartner calls this the Magic Square [21]. Although the aims and techniques of these approaches have similarities with our goals, there is also an important difference. We want to provide structured input for a running program instead of creating entire programs by a low-code editor. In the low-code approach, the input is typically composed by drag and drop while we use drop-down menus. The drag and drop approach seems more flexible, but Sect. 3.4 shows how one can insert new subexpressions in the existing input is such a way that all the input remains well-typed. With drag and drop it is much easier to make incorrect inputs.

The Hazel system tries to achieve a similar goal for text-based editors [12]. The typed holes of Hazel correspond with the typed recursive calls of our dynamic editor. The problem of unsolved overloading in the editor is handled similarly; the user of the system indicates the type required. The Hazel system has a very limited number of example languages, while the dynamic editors offer a frame work that is easy to use for new DSLs.

The LRC system was could create spreadsheet like editors based on attribute grammars [17]. The generated editors were more basic since it was in the early days of the web development.

9 Conclusion

Domain experts need the guidance of an editor to create complex well-typed inputs for their programs. In this paper, we investigate how we can create web-editors for this situation in an easy way. For plain first-order datatypes the generic mechanism of the iTask system can derive those editors automatically using datatype-generic programming. This is a very powerful technique since the programmer only has to define appropriate datatypes. The associated web-editors guarantee that only proper instances of those type can be made by the end-user and are obtained for free. The generic mechanism is limited to datatypes without functions, phantom types, existentially quantified variables.

For more advanced input languages the datatypes that can be handled by the generic system do not offer enough control. For instance, there is either no overloading in the input DSL or it is not type-safe. Also, the proper binding and type of user-defined identifiers in the DSL cannot be guaranteed. It is well-known how to handle such DSLs safely in functional programs. Common solutions are adding additional type information in phantom types, GADTs or in the functions of a shallow embedding. Unfortunately, the datatype generic system is not capable to handle any of those features.

For context sensitive restrictions like the selection of well-typed identifiers of given type even the known type systems are insufficient. The same holds for selecting known objects, like a ship or port from the current context. The static type systems of strongly typed languages like Clean has no knowledge about the existing objects at runtime.

The only option is to define the web-editors by hand. In this paper, we introduce dynamic editors that can handle all of the required features to make the input DSL type-safe. In such a dynamic editor the programmer specifies the drop-down menu of the editor by a list of dynamic edit elements. Each element contains a label shown to the user and a function controlling its behaviour. In any situation, the system only reveals the options that will produce a value of the required type to the end-user. A new instance of the dynamic web-editor is used to create the arguments of this function. The functions in those web-editor elements are perfectly suited to model the types needed in a type-safe editor for input DSLs.

We demonstrated how dynamic editors can be used to handle overloading, identifiers and extendable expressions in very convenient ways. Throughout the paper, we use a query language over ships, ports and wind-parks as a non-trivial example. This shows the limitations of deriving editors as well as how this DSL can be edited safely in dynamic editors with phantom types, GADTs and in a shallow embedding. This confirms that the dynamic editor system can solve all of the mentioned problems of standard web-editors and is a very useful extension of the iTask system. The dynamic editors are implemented as a special form of the default web-editors in iTask. This ensures that they can be incorporated in any desired way with the existing system. However, the architecture of dynamic editors is not limited to the iTask system. The implementation technique can potentially be used to specify editors in any system.

Dynamic editors scale very well, they are used in real world applications such as VIIA. VIIA helps guarding coasts, ports, windmill area's on sea, offshore platforms and the like. VIIA uses a large number of different Vessel Information tracking streams. Its end-users can be automatically warned when certain situations occur, for instance when a vessel is at risk (e.g. collision) or poses a risk (e.g. piracy, smuggling). These risks can be formulated by dynamic queries using the editors outlined here, see top-software.com.

Acknowledgements. Many thanks to the anonymous referees of this paper and our colleagues from the Radboud university and TOP-software for their feedback and support during this research. The techniques described here are first applied in VIIA that is developed in close collaboration with the Dutch Coastguard.

References

1. Achten, P., Alimarine, A., Plasmeijer, R.: When generic functions use dynamic values. In: Peña, R., Arts, T. (eds.) IFL 2002. LNCS, vol. 2670, pp. 17–33. Springer, Heidelberg (2001). https://doi.org/10.1007/3-540-44854-3_2
2. Achten, P., Koopman, P., Plasmeijer, R.: An introduction to task oriented programming. In: Zsók, V., Horváth, Z., Csató, L. (eds.) CEFP 2013. LNCS, vol. 8606, pp. 187–245. Springer, Cham (2015). https://doi.org/10.1007/978-3-319-15940-9_5
3. Achten, P.: Clean for Haskell98 programmers - a quick reference guide, July 13 2007. http://www.mbsd.cs.ru.nl/publications/papers/2007/achp2007-CleanHaskellQuickGuide.pdf
4. Alimarine, A., Plasmeijer, R.: A generic programming extension for clean. In: Arts, T., Mohnen, M. (eds.) IFL 2001. LNCS, vol. 2312, pp. 168–185. Springer, Heidelberg (2002). https://doi.org/10.1007/3-540-46028-4_11
5. Cheney, J., Hinze, R.: A lightweight implementation of generics and dynamics. In: Proceedings of the 2002 ACM SIGPLAN Haskell Workshop, June 2004
6. Gordon, A., Peyton Johnes, S.: LAMBDA: the ultimate excel worksheet function (2021). https://www.microsoft.com/en-us/research/blog/lambda-the-ultimatae-excel-worksheet-function/
7. HaskellWiki: Applications and libraries/GUI libraries – HaskellWiki (2019). https://wiki.haskell.org/index.php?title=Applications_and_libraries/GUI_libraries&oldid=63014. Accessed 6 Apr 2020
8. Hinze, R.: Memo functions, polytypically! In: Proceedings of the 2nd Workshop on Generic Programming, Ponte de, pp. 17–32 (2000)
9. Hughes, J.: Restricted data types in Haskell. In: Proceedings of the 1999 Haskell Workshop (1999)
10. Jones, W., Field, T., Allwood, T.: Deconstraining dsls (2012). https://doi.org/10.1145/2364527.2364571
11. Mestanogullari, A., Hahn, S., Arni, J.K., Löh, A.: Type-level web APIs with servant: an exercise in domain-specific generic programming. In: Proceedings of the 11th ACM SIGPLAN Workshop on Generic Programming, pp. 1–12. ACM (2015)
12. Omar, C., Voysey, I., Hilton, M., Aldrich, J., Hammer, M.A.: Hazelnut: a bidirectionally typed structure editor calculus. SIGPLAN Not. **52**(1), 86–99 (2017). https://doi.org/10.1145/3093333.3009900
13. Pil, M.: Dynamic types and type dependent functions. In: Hammond, K., Davie, T., Clack, C. (eds.) IFL 1998. LNCS, vol. 1595, pp. 169–185. Springer, Heidelberg (1999). https://doi.org/10.1007/3-540-48515-5_11
14. Plasmeijer, R., Lijnse, B., Michels, S., Achten, P., Koopman, P.: Task-oriented programming in a pure functional language. In: Proceedings of the 14th PPDP Symposium, pp. 195–206. ACM (2012). https://doi.org/10.1145/2370776.2370801

15. Plasmeijer, R., van Eekelen, M.: Clean language report (2012). https://clean.cs.ru. nl/Documentation
16. Richardson, C., Rymer, J.R.: New development platforms emerge for customer-facing applications (2014). www.forrester.com
17. Saraiva, J., Swierstra, D.: Generating spreadsheet-like tools from strong attribute grammars. In: Pfenning, F., Smaragdakis, Y. (eds.) Generative Programming and Component Engineering, pp. 307–323 (2003)
18. Schrijvers, T., Peyton Jones, S., Sulzmann, M., Vytiniotis, D.: Complete and decidable type inference for GADTs. In: Proceedings of the 14th ACM SIGPLAN ICFP, ICFP 2009, pp. 341–352. ACM (2009). https://doi.org/10.1145/1596550.1596599
19. Snoyman, M.: Developing Web Apps with Haskell and Yesod. O'Reilly Media, Sebastopol (2015)
20. team, H.: Happstack. happstack.com. Accessed 6 Apr 2020
21. Vincent, P., Lijjima, K., Driver, M., Wong, J., Natis, Y.: Magic quadrant for enterprise low-code application platforms (2019). www.gartner.com
22. Wikipedia contributors: Low-code development platform – Wikipedia (2020). https://en.wikipedia.org/w/index.php?title=Low-code_development_platform& oldid=944262991. Accessed 14 Mar 2020

Modelling, Translating, Proving
Functional Programs

High-Level Modelling for Typed Functional Programming

Yusuf Moosa Motara$^{(\boxtimes)}$ ⓘ

Department of Computer Science, Rhodes University, Makhanda 6140, South Africa
y.motara@ru.ac.za

Abstract. There is currently no way to model the high-level structural design of a functional system. Given the strong links between functional programming and mathematics, it is hypothesised that the language of mathematics can provide insight into how a functional system might be modelled. The approach is successful and both philosophy and the language of mathematics are used to identify the necessary modelling concepts and briefly outline some modelling notation alongside a small case study.

Keywords: Modelling · Structural modelling · Functional programming · Type model

1 Introduction

The structural design of functional systems—i.e., those written in a functional programming language, and/or obeying the conventions of the functional paradigm—cannot be modelled: neither modelling notation nor tools exist for this purpose. This paper contributes to addressing that research gap.

At the outset, the breadth of the research gap should be understood: there is no standard notation to model either typed or untyped functional systems at a high level, behaviorally or structurally. This is not to claim that no notation whatsoever exists: on the contrary, many ad-hoc notations exist (see, for example, the pages of [22,44], and many other such works), and different kinds of diagrams such as UML's Process Diagram or BPMN have been repurposed to fit the needs of the moment. None of these notations claim to be able to model functional systems *in general*, because they cannot. There remains, therefore, no standard way to model the structure of a functional system.

This work is part of a broader effort to allow functional programs to be modelled in an intuitive way. It focuses specifically on the *structural* modelling of *typed* functional programs at a *high level* and proposes a general, standard notation that should be applicable to all functional languages.

Computation in an object-oriented language is based on the idea that progress is made through communication between objects, each of which collaborates to achieve the goal of the system. By contrast, computation in a typed

V. Zsók and J. Hughes (Eds.): TFP 2021, LNCS 12834, pp. 69–94, 2021.
https://doi.org/10.1007/978-3-030-83978-9_4

functional language is based on the idea that values are transformed through pure functions, potentially resulting in a final value that is the end goal of the system[1].

There are several important features of a typed functional system which are either difficult or impossible to model using structural UML diagrams. These features are present in most typed functional languages. UML's *enumerations* are insufficiently powerful to represent sum types since the cases of such types are often linked to other data; the Composite design pattern has to be used instead. There is no good notation for modelling the functional semantics at the heart of functional programming, including lambda functions, nested functions, higher-order functions, partially-applied functions, composed functions, and closures. Most importantly, every structural UML diagram implicitly or explicitly requires some mapping of the domain to the idea of class- or object-like containers which are not necessarily present in functional languages. This means that while UML can be used to represent a wide range of systems, including real-world systems that do not involve computers, it must model them primarily as *entities* with relationships rather than as *operations* that involve entities. The underlying problem may be that the philosophy underlying such diagrams is fundamentally object-based [41].

The relationship between functional programming and modelling is a fundamentally mathematical one. This is in contrast to the relationship between object-oriented programming and modelling, which may be described as thoroughly pragmatic. The dominant object-oriented modelling language, UML, was created through a process of consensus and refinement [**bezivin_uml_1999**] and links to mathematics [11] or an underlying philosophy [12] have involved a great deal of retroactive patching. By contrast, the roots of functional programming are found in the lambda calculus [3], a mathematical description of what it means to compute. The combination of typing (via the Hindley-Milner type system [25]) led to the development of typed functional programming based on rigorous type theory [2].

The contributions of this work are as follows:

- A strong philosophical grounding is sought, found, and mapped between the language of mathematics and typed functional programming;
- A set of concepts common to all typed functional programming and not tied to any specific language are identified;
- A high-level structural modelling notation is briefly described, along with a small case study to demonstrate applicability.

The remainder of this paper is structured as follows. Section 2 justifies the approach used to search for a modelling solution. Section 3 discusses modelling, and explicitly situates and scopes the work within a particular modelling context. Section 4 looks at related work. A philosophical basis is laid out in Sect. 5 and an exploration of mathematical language is found in Sect. 6. The philosophy and language are combined in Sect. 7 to identify a set of concepts for modelling.

---

[1] Event-based functional languages, such as Elm, omit the idea of a final value.

A notation for modelling these concepts is first theoretically justified and then proposed (Sect. 8). A short case study is presented in Sect. 9 and conclusions are drawn in Sect. 10.

2   Approach

The majority of this paper traverses the ground of philosophy, language, mathematical discourse, and design—with a case study at the end. It takes time to build bridges between these areas and explain them in sufficient detail for our purposes. Why should such a long and winding path be taken, rather than simply finding some notation that looks usable and causes practitioners to nod their heads?

The design of systems is ultimately a purposeful activity: every system has some reason for existing, even if that reason is a purely exploratory one. This design will typically follow the ways of thought that have been developed by the designer [33], and will often be restricted by those ways of thought as well [4]. It is therefore of primary importance to ensure that system stakeholders are encouraged to think in a way that facilitates a design which can easily be encoded as a computer system, and which discourages ways of thinking which are difficult to encode. Three categories of common design-related thinking are categorized here:

1. Thinking in a problem domain. A person may think of a problem in terms of their field of specialization, such as accounting or botany, or in terms of some other influence, such as fishing or family discussions. The ease of translation into a computer system is dependent on the degree to which system language(s) are able to encode the original thinking.
2. Thinking in a programming language. A developer may think of a problem in terms that a language makes available to them. Ease of translation into a computer system is assured, but the degree to which that system reflects the actual problem domain will be relative to how accurately the problem domain can be expressed in the language. A further issue is that a design of this type may be inaccessible to stakeholders without the requisite technical knowledge.
3. Thinking in a notation. A stakeholder—whether developer, business analyst, or other person—may think of a problem in terms that a notation supports. Ease of translation is into a computer system is related to the ease with which notational semantics are translatable into computational semantics, and the degree to which the system reflects the actual problem domain is relative to how accurately the problem domain can be expressed in the notation [35].

Domain-specific languages may successfully be used to bridge (1) and (2) [18], but introduce problems of their own and should therefore not be used without due consideration [24, p. 320]. It is category (3) that is most accessible to the widest audience, and which this paper is concerned with. However, the accessibility of this category introduces problems of its own since stakeholders must use the same underlying philosophy to be able to participate in any modelling process that uses the notation. That philosophy is, in the object-oriented world, provided by an underlying theory of objects [40]—although the details of what an "object" itself is have been contested [1]. Without a shared underlying philosophy, it is argued that stakeholders will have difficulty conceptualizing their ideas notationally and will become frustrated with a notation rather than using it effectively.

An appropriate philosophical backing for modelling is important [12], and deep concern for philosophy when proposing a high-level model is not simply theoretical: it is rooted in our field's history [10, p. 73]:

> Most of our current 'modelling languages' (MLs) date back to the 1990s and therefore claim to be 'general purpose'—a prime example being the Unified Modeling Language (UML) from the Object Management Group (OMG) [9]. Although claiming to support a wide range of modelling abstraction levels (i.e. analysis and design) in the one package, its history of development clearly indicates that it is highly focussed towards (low-level or detailed) design and even implementation (e.g. Java and C++-style concepts are evident). Some Domain-Specific Modelling Languages (DSMLs) show the same bias, when presented as a 'UML Profile'.

(references in original). The core issue here is that languages *currently* popular should not have an outsize impact on notation that may outlive them; without the stabilizing influence of an explicit underlying philosophy, the link between notation and language becomes contaminated by specific language constructs. What looks "usable" or "familiar" today is often a function of the programmer's experience and should not be discounted, but should not be considered as a sufficient reason for particular notation to exist.

The link between problem domain and notation is also an area of concern. If the notation makes it easy to model the problem domain in a way that is unsuitable for implementation, conflict ensues [35, p. 238]:

> [I]t was not just that UML contained semantic ambiguities and inconsistencies, but rather that the increased prominence given to particular modelling notations had in turn placed a premium on carrying out certain kinds of analysis and design activity. Analysts were enthusiastically adopting new approaches to conceptualising their system, eventually becoming trapped in unproductive arguments over the objects populating the system and the proper representation of the control structure of the system. Designers were then refusing to implement the models produced by the analysts, since it was often impossible to map from use case models and sequence diagrams onto anything that a conventional software engineer would recognise.

Once again, such issues could be mitigated with reference to some shared underlying philosophy that guides analysis, design, and implementation.

Finding a suitable underlying philosophy and creating a conceptual bridge to link problem domain, language, and notation is seen as a way of avoiding some of the difficulties that attended the birth, development, and use of UML. The specific notation itself, as an artifact of this search, is relatively unimportant as long as *some* viable notation can be demonstrated. This is not stated to dismiss the importance of a concrete notation, but to elevate the importance of its foundation. By analogy, one can say that any specific software system is relatively unimportant when compared to the importance of the principles of software design which guided its creation and the creation of thousands of other software systems.

Furthermore, researchers with access to the underlying foundation of a notation are free to propose other notation that is based upon it, and that notation is likely to be coherent with—or superior to—what is proposed in this paper. Researchers are also free to critique, supplement, and revise the foundation, thus making for a firmer foundation for future notation. However, researchers *without* access to the foundation of a notation must simply guess at the philosophical underpinnings and linkages by working backwards from the notation, leading to unnecessary misunderstandings and unproductive competing proposals on implicit grounds of language-preference, problem-domain utility, and so on.

3   Modelling Context

Models obtain their power through their ability to "be used in place of what they model" [28]. This is most often a system which is part of a larger domain of interest which, itself, is part of the totality of reality [11]. A useful general modelling language should be able to model many domains of interest and, ideally, much of reality. This aligns well with the idea of a general programming language, while not detracting from the importance and utility of specialist modelling languages and programming languages.

Models may be either structural or behavioural. A structural model expresses the elements of a model that exist and the way in which elements of the model relate to each other. A behavioural model expresses the way in which a system accomplishes a task. This work is concerned with structural modelling only. With that said, the term "structural" may also encompass behavioral aspects of a functional system. This is because functional programming is declarative, and describing the relationships between declarations also goes some way towards expressing how a task is accomplished. Nevertheless, the distinction between behavioural and structural is a useful one since it excludes models which focus primarily on behaviour rather than structure.

A model may be used as either a description or a specification [28]. The distinction is in where the truth of the system lies: in the former case, it is with the system, and in the latter case, it is with the model. Many excellent specification languages already exist for the functional paradigm (e.g. [15,29]), and this work attempts to be complementary to these. It proposes, therefore, a descriptive modelling language. This does not preclude a role similar to that of a specification since a descriptive model which is developed earlier in the development process may be used as a prescriptive model—a loose specification, if so desired—and can be regarded as having a more descriptive role during and after development [28].

Following on from Stachowiak [37] as reported by Kühne [19], a model must have the qualities of mapping, reduction, and pragmatism: it must be based on some system ("mapping"), reflect only the relevant parts of that system ("reduction"), and be usable in place of the original system with respect to some purpose ("pragmatism"). Kühne simplifies both mapping and reduction under the term "projection", and sets out the view that abstraction may be described through function composition [19, p. 371]:

$$\alpha = \tau \circ \alpha' \circ \pi$$

Model abstraction (α) consists of projection (π), some further abstraction (α') on elements (including relationships), and a translation τ to another representation, i.e., the modelling language. With projection π we associate any filtering of elements both reducing their number and individual information content.

Given some actual system S and some notation N, with an abstract model M, one can think of these as having the types $\alpha : S \to N$, $\pi : S \to M$, $\alpha' : M \to M$, and $\tau : M \to N$.

The "further abstraction (α')" aspect requires additional explanation: why is it required? Kühne explains the necessity by differentiating between two kinds of model:

- **Token models** are those where there is "a one-to-one correspondence between relationships and elements in the model $\mathcal{M}$ and a subset of these in system $\mathcal{S}$" [19, p. 373]. Token models can therefore be used as direct representations for the actual system, and this remains true even when token models refer to other token models, or when the "mapping" part of projection elides or combines some of the finer details of the actual system. Token models capture the system-specific aspects of a system. A blueprint, for example, is a token model.
- **Type models** are those which operate by trait-classification rather than by replication and/or combination of a system's elements. A trait may be identified, from an object-oriented point-of-view, with a UML interface in a class diagram: it specifies which behaviours should be present *without* specifying which specific class or properties must be used to provide those behaviours. It therefore captures "*universal* aspects of a system's elements by means of *classification*" [19, p. 374] (emphasis in original).

In a token model, the α' function is unnecessary since projection is sufficient; there is no further abstraction and one can regard α' as being the identity function. In a type model, however, the α' function serves to classify elements and relationships prior to translation. The proposed modelling language in this work aims to show a high-level design-oriented view, and is therefore closer to a type model than a token model.

Lastly, a model must have a particular intention: a reason for existing or a purpose that it must be fit for. The intention of a model is "a mixture of requirements, behavior, properties, and constraints, either satisfied or maintained by the [model]" [28, p. 350]. The intention of the proposed notation is to allow a modeller to express the underlying design of a system in a way that is comprehensible to others.

In summary, a model created using the notation described in this work would be structural; applicable to many domains of interest; descriptive; type-model focused; and aimed at exposing a comprehensible system design.

4   Related Work

This section has been split into two subsections. The first of these considers the applicability of mainstream modelling languages which were developed without considering either functional programming or its mathematical basis. The second broadens the related work to consider mathematically-oriented notations and notations which have been specifically designed with functional languages in mind.

4.1   Mainstream Modelling Languages

UML's behavioural diagrams are more useful for representing the semantic structure of a functional program. The Interaction and State diagrams, in particular, are easy to adapt for the structural modelling of simple functional systems. Interaction diagrams could be used to represent functions as blocks, with labeled data going between them; conversely, State diagrams could be used to represent data as blocks, with labeled functions joining them. These diagrams do not scale: more complicated systems involving sum types with four or more cases quickly become a nightmare of lines, diamonds, and boxes.

There are other diagrams which are meant to represent processes, albeit in more limited contexts. Two of the most popular of these notations are Process Diagrams [30] from Business Process Modeling Notation (BPMN) and Data Flow Diagrams (DFDs). Both DFDs and Process Diagrams are behavioural models rather than structural models: they specify the way in which data flows between entities, rather than the relationships between entities themselves. As behavioural diagrams for functional programming, they have some merit; for example, the restrictions on how processes may be used at the sentence level map admirably to the way in which functions operate [21, p. 86]:

> Processes cannot consume or create data. That means the process must have at least 1 input data flow (to avoid miracles), at least 1 output data flow (to avoid black holes) and should have sufficient inputs to create outputs (to avoid gray holes).

Nevertheless, both DFDs and Process Diagrams make function-type inputs or outputs difficult to represent naturally. The former is better at this than the latter since a DFD is to be viewed in conjunction with a Data Dictionary wherein the relevant function-type can be given a suitable name. Although this may be adequate, it is not necessarily a good fit since function inputs and outputs are very important and, ideally, should not be relegated to a separate document.

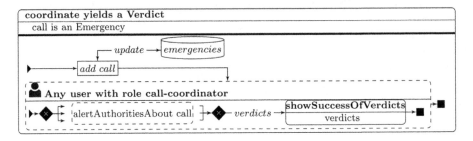

Fig. 1. Example of Tonic graphical notation (reproduced from [38, p. 36])

Tonic visualisations [38], inspired by BPMN and developed as the complement of GiN [13], are a specific adaptation that targets task-oriented programming (see Fig. 1) and are suitable for expressing aspects of functional programming.

4.2   Functional Programming and Modelling

Due to its mathematical roots, functional programmers have tended to use mathematics as the most intuitive and general modelling tool at their disposal. Category theory [23] provides a visual way to represent and reason about arrows and objects which are analogous to functions and types in a typed functional programming language. However, this visualisation is suitable only for considering functions and types, and there is no obvious way to extend its scope. Figure 2 demonstrates this by reproducing a representative figure from [23, p. 16]. It succinctly defines what a natural transformation $\tau : S \rightarrow T$ looks like by relating the categories S and T, but its ability to describe the domain itself has not been tested. The most promising works in this direction are likely [6] and [36] which try to make category theory accessible to others, enabling them to "think in categories" in the same way that budding programmers are encouraged to "think in objects". While this is certainly a worthwhile goal, it nevertheless keeps functional programming opaque to those who have *not* been taught to think in such a way. Modelling is a complementary way to improve the accessibility of functional programming.

Motara [27] suggests a novel way to use string diagrams [34] to represent lower-level function manipulation. Their work focuses on behavioral modelling and the syntax and semantics are not applicable to structural modelling. Other

$$
\begin{array}{ccc}
c & S_c \xrightarrow{\ \tau_c\ } T_c \\
\downarrow{\scriptstyle f} & \downarrow{\scriptstyle S_f} \quad \downarrow{\scriptstyle T_f} \\
c', & S_{c'} \xrightarrow{\ \tau_{c'}\ } T_{c'}
\end{array}
$$

Fig. 2. Modelling in category theory

works which use string diagrams are [14] and [34] where they are used to increase the accessibility of category-theoretical manipulations in a novel way. An alternative graphical approach is taken by Eklund [5] in a paper which is focused on understanding monadic composition. Once again, however, all these cannot readily be extended to the modelling that is desired in this work.

Type-driven development and domain-driven design, as exemplified by [8,44] for functional languages, model within a programming language. They pragmatically take advantage of type systems to explicate a domain, creating small domain-specific languages that map naturally to the domain that is being modeled. While this style of modelling is successful, there is no common notation for it and it is sometimes only accessible to developers rather than a broader audience (see, for example, Chapter 4 of [8]).

5   Philosophical Underpinnings

A late-Wittgensteinian [43] language-centric approach will be taken as a philosophical basis. This approach was selected based on Wittgenstein's language-centric and context-dependent view of problems and philosophy. This view, it could be argued, is a good fit for the functional paradigm since functional designs often strongly emphasise language use: see, for example, [9,16,32]. Furthermore, Wittgenstein's later philosophy is well-regarded in philosophical circles [20] and has the benefit of having been examined and analysed for over half a century. Such a philosophical foundation is more likely to be stable than one which is created ad-hoc for a particular goal.

Wittgenstein's philosophy can be broken up into "early" and "late" eras, with the early Wittgenstein approach finding its zenith in the *Tractatus Logico-Philosophicus* [42]. Later Wittgenstein turned away from significant aspects of the earlier work and can be most clearly seen in *Philosophical Investigations* [43], which forms the basis of this summary. That work is written as a series of numbered paragraphs and, for the purposes of this work, it is only necessary to consider paragraphs up to ≈140.

Philosophical Investigations is written as a response to both the attempted formalization of language into strict logical propositions and to the broader consideration of what constitutes philosophy itself. Wittgenstein therefore writes about language itself, how it is constructed, and how it is meant. To assist a reader who wishes to consider the source material, the original numbered paragraphs from [43] which form the basis of each part of this summary are included in parentheses for the remainder of this section.

In Wittgenstein's estimation the fundamental starting-point is to consider language not as words strung together within a grammatical framework, but as moves within a *language-game*. A language-game is the "game" of communication that sets up a context within which language is used and within which one party or another may make "moves", and within which there are many varieties of expression (23). For example, the word "fire" has a very different meaning depending on whether one is in a crowded movie theatre or at a shooting range or in a Human Resources meeting. Similarly, a word may be a command or a question or something else entirely, with its meaning hinging on expression or tone or something else (21); and how we categorise words depends upon both the aim of the classification and upon our own subjectivity (17). Within a language-game, the meaning of a sentence is more important than the way in which the sentence is constructed and, indeed, two sentences or words which mean the same thing but are otherwise different should be considered to be the same (20, 24, 138). All language-games depend on implicit presuppositions (31) which may naturally be assumed given strong enough evidence (33) for them. A word by itself, depending on the situation in which it is used, may be a sentence on its own (49).

Language-games may include names. A name *signifies* a thing, but is not that thing, much as the name-tag which is attached to a thing is not the thing itself (15, 40). A name continues to exist because the meaning of a name continues to exist, even if the bearer of the name no longer exists (41, 55). This aspect of language allows us to talk about bearers which have been destroyed. A name has no meaning whatsoever outside of a particular language-game, and the mere naming of something is not—until the name is used—a move in a language-game (49). Since all names have a meaning which must necessarily exist for them to be used within their language-game, it makes no sense to talk about whether a name "exists" or not (50, 57, 58). The meaning behind a name, and how to use it, must necessarily be known before a name is defined (31). Similarly to names, all words in a language game are ways to represent other things (50).

Demonstratives (such as "that" and "here") are a special case of words which require a bearer; however, this fact alone does not make a demonstrative into a name (9, 45). Each language-game may contain words that have specific uses within that game (10, 11, 43), and very little is gained by considering them to be more similar than they are (14).

There is nothing that is natively composite, outside of a particular language-game (47). Even within a particular language-game, what is "composite" may defined variously as the game progresses (48). What is important is not the "simplified" or "composite" forms of things, howsoever they may be defined, but the avoidance of misunderstandings (48) since there may be times when a "simplified" form (e.g. "brush and stick") is neither more fundamental nor more simple than the "composite" form (e.g. "broom") (60–63); but this depends, ultimately, on the language-game that is in use (64).

An inexact meaning is still eminently usable, and the drawing of boundaries around it does not necessarily make it more useful, except in the more specialized case where a word has a niche meaning that is amenable to such boundaries being drawn (69, 81, 139). It is often context or examples—the manner in which it is used—which make the meaning most clear (29, 71). Meanings should therefore be separated only to the extent that, within the language-game, they are needed to avoid misunderstanding (87, 88, 98, 99). A word may have many meanings, each of which independently support the word, and no fixed meaning (77, 79, 87); and the same word, used in a different way, may result in a different meaning (140).

All philosophical problems are, in fact, problems of language (109). These arise because philosophers insist on trying to understand concepts and words— such as "truth", "world", and "self"—in isolation and divorced from any language-game, which is precisely where they are most meaningless (105–108). Instead, philosophers should restrict themselves to describing (and never explaining) things within the context of their language-game (109, 125); this is the only way in which problems may be solved. Any such solution is one way in which a problem may be solved, but not necessarily the only way (131, 132), and is not generalisable to largely-unrelated cases (133).

6 The Language of Mathematics

The Language of Mathematics [7] demonstrates a way in which arbitrary symbolic and textual mathematics, as written in standard works and textbooks, can be parsed, understood, and represented with full semantics using Discourse Representation Theory [17]. Critically, the work uses linguistic theory to understand mathematics as a language and then encode it within a modified Discourse Representation Structure (DRS). Such a DRS is capable of translating and encoding the lambda calculus [3], the basis of all functional programming, as well as type-theoretic logic [2]. *The Language of Mathematics* identifies as many features of natural-language mathematics as possible, and strives to find an encoded form of those features without loss of semantics. This work takes precisely the opposite approach and asks: if we consider a functional representation to be the encoded form of a system, is it possible to obtain a more natural language form without loss of semantics?

6.1 Natural Language Structure

For the convenience of the reader, certain terms will be written in **boldface**. These terms are those which will be particularly important in later discussion.

One apparent difference between mathematical language and a program is that mathematics is typically written either in the form of an argument, with various statements bolstering some conclusions or results, or in the form of an exploration where background knowledge is described. These two forms map neatly to the ideas of a functional program and a functional library respectively: the former makes at least one argument about inputs and transformations and outputs, and the latter describes tools that may be used in the course of such an argument.

Mathematical language is written in one of two **modes**: formal and informal. Formal statements are possible to evaluate objectively. Informal statements, such as "It is *interesting* that the Fibonacci sequence appears in many natural contexts", give opinions but are not subject to computational evaluation.

Mathematical language may be textual—expressed in English[2]—and/or symbolic, with symbols being used "to abbreviate material that would be too cumbersome to state with text alone" [7, p. 17]. Symbols are often **embedded** within textual material and their **abbreviative** use makes it much easier to convey complex ideas in a small amount of space; indeed, the argument is made that "modern mathematics would quickly become unreadable" [7, p. 18] without such use of symbols. Symbols which represent terms can be embedded in contexts that accept a noun, and symbolic formulae can be embedded in contexts that accept a clause or sentence. Symbolic terms often carry **presuppositions**; for example, "'$\sqrt{x}$' presupposes that x has a square root, i.e. that x is nonnegative" [7, p. 31], assuming that a real-valued solution is desired.

An important feature of mathematical language is **adaptivity**: the way in which the textual and/or symbolic lexicons are updated with more nuanced meanings as additional mathematical definitions are encountered. For example, $\frac{3}{4}$ may initially be understood as "three parts out of a four-part whole", but may later be understood to also mean "three divided among four entities" when the appropriate mathematical definitions are encountered. This also brings into focus the critical importance of **definitions** in mathematical language.

Mathematical prose is commonly organized into blocks. The most important blocks used in mathematical language appear to be:

- **Lemma**, denoting a minor result that is useful on the path to a greater goal;
- **Definition**, which updates textual and/or symbolic lexicons;
- **Theorem**, denoting a major and important result;
- **Proposition**, denoting a result that is more important than a Lemma, but less important than a Theorem;
- **Corollary**, denoting a consequence that naturally follows from the truth of a Lemma, Theorem, or Proposition.

Blocks are often numbered so that they can be referred to unambiguously from other parts of an argument. "Proof" blocks, denoting the means by which a "lemma", "theorem", or "proposition" are shown to be true, exist only as part of these other blocks. "Proof" blocks are only used to separate the result from reasoning and are not numbered. Such a block is therefore more usefully regarded as a part of one of the other named blocks than as having an independent existence. Most blocks represent the *behavioral* component of mathematical text and make an argument that links the entities from "Definition" blocks together.

Mathematical blocks often involve the use of **variables**. These are used as a form of anaphor[3] and are often scoped to the block itself. It is asserted that

---

[2] Or other natural language.

[3] The use of words to refer to other entities without naming them, e.g. "The lady ate food that *she* enjoyed". Pronouns are a form of anaphor.

"[t]hey cannot be eliminated precisely because anaphor is not powerful enough to replace them" [7, p. 31] and this observation is likely to be true in the case of a functional system as well.

A careful reading of [7] reveals several intra-block formal-mode mathematical rhetorical constructs beyond (and including) those obviously classed as rhetorical (see [7, p. 77–82]). The identified rhetorical constructs are:

- **Variable definition**. Variables are often defined intensionally (i.e. by predicate). *Examples*: "Let $x \in \mathbb{N}$"; "Let K be a ring".
- **Naming**. This names a particularly important result, often a Theorem, so that it can be referred to by name. *Example*: "Theorem 2.4 'Sigmund's Paradox'".
- **Presupposition**. This is used to attach a restriction to the use of a construct. *Example*: "$\sqrt{n}$ is defined for all $n \geq 0$".
- **Consequence**. This qualifies the condition(s) under which a definition is true. *Example*: "If $I \times A = A$ and $A \times I = A$, then I is the identity matrix".
- **Cross-reference**. This is used to refer unambiguously to a result demonstrated elsewhere. *Example*: "By Sigmund's Paradox (Theorem 2.4), ...".
- **Conclusion**. This is the final result of a Lemma, Proposition, or Theorem.
- **Product type**. This creates a named grouping. *Example*: "A polite sentence P consists of a subject, a predicate, and a politeness modifier".
- **Sum type**. This creates a discrete, named set of elements. *Example*: "We say that 2, 3, 5, 7, and 11 are members of the set of initial primes Q".

Note that common sentences such as "Given a set of sets S, the powerset $P(S)$ is the set of all subsets of S" may contain more than one of the identified constructs.

7   The Bridge over the River Wittgenstein

A bridge between *The Language of Mathematics* (LoM) and typed functional programming (TFP) will be created in this section, using *Philosophical Investigations* (PI) to go between the two. The intermediary philosophical link is crucial for being able to take ideas from one side to the other in a principled and theoretically justifiable way. LoM presents a coherent and clear account of mathematical language; PI provides a coherent and clear account of natural language. To the best of the author's knowledge, there is no comparable account for TFP, and attempting to establish one *a priori* risks creating a biased design based on the author's subjective experiences with functional languages.

Whenever possible, the link should not be made *directly* between TFP and LoM because this risks conflating the former with the latter. While the two may be similar, they are not the same, and pretending that they are serves no purpose. PI serves as a guard against this tendency and forces the modelling to be done on the level of a human-focused language-game. Conversely, attempting to establish a typed functional programming language-game with only the philosophy of language-games makes misclassification errors more likely and unnecessarily discards the touchstone of mathematics. Anaphora, for example, may be sought and "found" in typed functional programming when variables [7, p. 31] are likely to be a more appropriate abstraction.

Mathematics cannot be fully understood out of its context or in an isolated way; the same is true of words in a language-game, and functions and types and their relationships in typed functional programming. PI describes many varieties of expression, and mathematics restricts itself to either the formal or informal. The closest analogue to an informal mode in TFP may be programming comments.

Wittgenstein's discussion of ambiguity can be broken down into (at least) the following distinct points:

1. A word may have many meanings, each of which support the word independently, or no fixed meaning.
2. A word may have an inexact meaning, as long as it can be distinguished from other words.
3. A word's meaning may change as the game progresses.

All of these are traits hold true in mathematics: for example, "prime" has many meanings, "interesting" has no fixed meaning, "abstract" may have an inexact meaning, and examples of adaptivity have already been given. In typed functional programming, the fold operation (and other parametrically polymorphic operations) can have many meanings, shadowing makes it possible for a name to have localized and global meanings, and the meaning of words such as "authorised" or "valid" may change as more moves are made. Yet, just as in the case of a language-game, essential meaning is preserved despite—and sometimes because of—ambiguity.

Mathematical blocks do not appear to have any explicitly described counterpart in the philosophy of language-games. However, *Philosophical Investigations* consists of numbered paragraphs which are set up such that they may reference each other, thus implicitly taking on a structure of blocks and cross-references. It can therefore be said that a paragraph is analogous to a block, and the structure of the text forms a presupposition [43, par. 31] that is important for the semantics of the text. On the mathematical side, the importance of blocks in structuring mathematical language is overwhelmingly clear: there are few mathematical texts that do *not* follow this convention, and cross-referencing between blocks is critical. Similarly, the importance of numbered paragraphs in Wittgenstein's own implicit language game is critical for cross-referencing purposes.

On the typed functional programming side, a plausible analogue is ostensibly the abstraction of packages/modules/namespaces which most languages have. This analogue is not without its problems, however: such containers may be used to package a wide variety of functionality from GUI components to algorithms to service interfaces. It seems unreasonable to insist that each of these forms is either the same as all the others, or to create distinctions—with no principled basis—between "kinds" of containers. There therefore appears to be no direct analogue for mathematical blocks.

Mathematical rhetoric is used to form sentences through which "moves" are made within the language-game of mathematical language. Rhetoric links blocks, which delineate an overall structure, and argumentation together, building on already-demonstrated results to develop a richer mathematical narrative. Types and functions perform a similar role in typed functional programming; see, for example, [44] where functions are used to transform types (and hence meaning) from more basic forms to more sophisticated ones. Types naturally encode rhetorical "sum type" and "product type" constructs, and functions naturally encode the rhetorical constructs of "presupposition" (as logic) and "conclusion" (as return values). However, simple functions and types do not allow one to express *general* narratives such as "Any valid calculation must remain within particular bounds". Parametrically polymorphic types, combined with functions that obey certain "laws" by convention, give rise to applicative functors, monads, and other such constructs. These constructs can be used to express richer narratives. Ironically, these constructs can also be formidable barriers to understanding. The fundamental issue, covered well in [31], is subtle but pervasive throughout typed functional programming: abstract knowledge of parametrically polymorphic functions and the transformations that they *potentially* enable is not sufficient to combine them sensibly or construct a cohesive narrative from them. The typed functional programming domain has many ways to describe functions and transformations (lambda, higher-order, functor, applicative, arrow, ...) but no way to describe how to link these into a cohesive narrative. The "moves" made by sophisticated typed functional narratives are difficult to discern because a *design*-relevant rhetoric to describe those moves is almost entirely missing.

Mathematical language uses variables instead of "demonstratives" and similar anaphora, but the typed functional paradigm lacks a similar exclusive way to identify other entities. Instead, features such as arguments, closed-over values, types, and namespacing are used to refer to particular kinds of entities in different contexts. A similar situation occurs when considering the idea of language-game names, which can be neatly mapped to textual/symbolic definitions in mathematical language. Typed functional programming defines multiple named entities such as named functions, types, and modules/packages, all of which may be used as names in different contexts.

7.1 Proposed Basis

The following principles were applied to arrive at a suitable TFP modelling language:

1. If similar language exists in LoM, PI, and TFP, then it is clearly important in all three and should be represented in modelling language for TFP.
2. If similar language exists in LoM and PI, but not in TFP, then it is likely to be part of a modelling vocabulary that must be developed for TFP and should be represented in a TFP modelling language.
3. If certain language exists only in LoM, then it is likely to have a use only in LoM and should not be included in a TFP modelling language.

4. If multiple expressions of a language construct exist in LoM, and fewer analogous expressions exist in PI and/or TFP, then it is possible that the expanded set of language constructs is only necessary in LoM because of the specific requirements of mathematics. On the basis that meanings should only be separated to the extent that this is necessary (see [43, par. 88, 89, 98, 99]), a reduced set of language constructs—ideally, only those which are necessitated by PI—should be represented in a TFP modelling context.

5. If multiple expressions of a language construct exist in TFP, and fewer analogous expressions exist in PI and/or LoM, then it is possible that the expanded set of language constructs is only necessary in TFP because of the specific requirements of TFP. This does not necessarily mean that such constructs are necessary in a *modelling* or design context. On the basis that meanings should only be separated to the extent that this is necessary, a reduced set of language constructs—ideally, only those which are necessitated by PI—should be represented in a TFP modelling context.

Principles (4) and (5) are the most controversial since the case could be made for an expanded TFP modelling language rather than a reduced one. Such a case has not been made because it is thought to be better to create a smaller initial language that can be expanded rather than a larger language that may later have constructs removed from it.

Recall that Kühne's model of abstraction [19] involves projection (π, consisting of both mapping and reduction), then further abstraction (α'), and lastly translation (τ) to the modelling language. This section jointly considers both π and α', with the goal of outlining a standardised design language and vocabulary which can later be translated into a modelling language. That translation must take into account additional design factors around notation—the "Physics of Notation" [26,39]—and will be presented in Sect. 8.

A majority of concepts and ideas can pass seamlessly, with a one-to-one correspondence, over the philosophical bridge that links LoM and TFP. A π function thus encompasses modes, symbols, definitions, and variables.

The following points sketch the outlines of a principled α':

1. High-level design rhetoric is almost entirely missing from TFP, but exists as sentences in both LoM and PI. Such rhetoric must be created, but much of it is used in LoM in a *behavioural* context and is not necessary for a *structural* model. Two rhetorical constructs, "sum" and "product" distinction, exist already in TFP.

2. The concept of structured blocks exists in LoM, but has an implicit existence as paragraphs in PI. The primary purpose of blocks in both is to separate and allow for easy cross-referencing. Relevant block structures must be created, and must be amenable to cross-referencing.

3. LoM variables and definitions both have multiple representations in TFP. They will be coalesced into the simpler representations from LoM.

A case has already been made for including definitions in the modelling basis. Natural analogues for other blocks were not found in typed functional programming, but some commonalities clearly exist between natural and mathematical language. The remaining blocks were therefore classified as follows:

- "Lemma", "proposition", and "theorem" blocks differ in the importance accorded to them and are also relatively hierarchical. While some natural language texts do contain such divisions, many others do not, and PI has little to say about them. It is plausible that they could be coalesced into a single construct.
- "Corollary" blocks exist in LoM, but have no explicit existence in PI. They should therefore be ignored.

8   Notation

The notation is guided by best-practice principles from the literature, which will be detailed first. The actual notation follows as a separate subsection.

8.1   Design Process

This work will use the Physics of Notation Systematized (PoN-S) design process [39], which aims to create workable artifacts that follow the principles of good notation suggested by Moody [26], and which is very briefly summarized below. Such principles aim to improve "the speed, ease, and accuracy with which a representation can be processed by the human mind" [26, p. 757].

The PoN-S process begins by looking at cognitive fit: whether the notation will fit the task and the audience.

Given a task and audience, the second step of PoN-S is to determine the symbols to be used in the notation. This involves three principles: semiotic clarity, semantic transparency, and perceptual discriminability. A symbol has semiotic clarity when it maps to one (or zero) concepts, and when each concept is mapped to a maximum of one symbol. Each symbol, by the principle of semantic transparency, should suggest its semantics; and each must be perceptually discriminable (i.e. visually distinguishable) from other symbols.

The symbols should ideally be enhanced to improve the speed, ease, and accuracy of their processing. This involves improving their visual expressiveness through the use of different visual characteristics (position, shape, size, colour, hue, orientation, and texture), limiting the number of symbols (graphic economy), and using text to improve the clarity and expressiveness of symbols (dual coding).

Lastly, PoN-S calls for identification of legitimate ways in which symbols may be combined. This specifically requires forethought about the complexity management of a notation: what looks reasonable for a few symbols may turn into a chaotic mess when hundreds or thousands of symbols are involved. A validation step then ends the PoN-S process.

8.2   Proposed Notation

Section 7.1 expands on both projection (π) and further abstraction (α'), leaving only translation (τ) to a notation to be considered. This section deals with that translation. The audience for the notation is *inter alia* students, developers, and business analysts; in other words, a broad and general audience which has some technical background and may be interested in software, software features, and software design, but may not necessarily be *au fait* with the details of software development. The task is to allow a typed functional system's structure to be expressed, modified, and understood by this audience.

For ease of reference in other works, this preliminary high-level notation can be called HL0 (pronounced "hello").

As discussed in Sect. 3, a structural model expresses the elements of a model that exist and the way in which elements of the model relate to each other. A model, in addition, must have the quality of pragmatism. This leads naturally to the question of which relationships one should express in order for the model to be useful. While there are many competing answers to this, a reasonable start might be to consider some common questions that people have about language in general, and attempt to model those relationships:

1. "What words exist, and what do they mean?" is answered by a dictionary.
2. "Which words are similar?" is answered by a thesaurus.
3. "What is the ancestry of this word?" is answered by a book of etymology.

Fig. 3. Notation for definition (left) and thesaurus (right)

The most significant notation is for definitions (see Fig. 3). The leftmost part of a definition is a *rub-'al-ḥizb*[4] shape which contains symbolic notation. The *rub-'al-ḥizb* is chosen not only for its distinctive visual appearance, but also because it is found at Unicode codepoint 06DE. This makes it easy to integrate into text when one wishes to use parametric polymorphism.

On the right of a definition, expandable space exists for textual definition. If an alphabetic name in the symbolic definition may be substitutable with something else, then it will appear in boldface in the textual definition. Textual definitions often contain the "▶" symbol which indicates different cases which are patterned on the definition, and which lead (via "→") to some mapped

---

[4] Pronounced "roob-El-Hizb", with emphasis on the capitalized letters. IPA: [ruːb ʕl hizb].

entity[5]. The ▶ is also used to indicate different cases in a sum type; if a product type exists, • would be used to describe the components of the group. A "_" symbol indicates a fall-through case.

Thesaurus notation (see Fig. 3) begins with a boldface title that describes the basis of the similarity. Each similar item is then listed in turn, with a short colon-prefixed description that expresses why it should be a member of the group.

Definitions should only make reference to definitions already defined above them, assuming a reading order of top-to-bottom and then left-to-right, and thesaurus elements should follow after all definitions. This causes symbols and their meanings to be (partially) ordered such that more basic definitions always precede more advanced ones: a *dictionary*. When one definition is a structural subset of another, effectively aliasing a particular part of the larger definition, then the subsidiary definition should be joined to its source by a diamond-terminated line: ◆———◇ . A suggested name for this is the "alias" relationship. When one definition is built upon another, the subsidiary definition should be joined to its basis by a circle-terminated line: ●———○. A suggested name for this is the "relies" relationship[6]. In both cases, the black side indicates the origin. Together, these lines show *etymology* relationships. When a definition has relationships to many other definitions, it is given a thick black border instead of lines to avoid clutter. This indicates that it is fundamental to the problem domain.

In terms of notational clarity, perceptual discriminability is ensured through distinctive shapes, position, colour, and graphic economy. Semiotic clarity is good, given that this is a type model and thus classifies by traits at a high level; the use of ⬡ and the shape of a symbolic definition enclosure relate ⬡ intuitively to "some definition".

Some symbols will have to be reserved by convention. The following subset of symbols covers all of the cases encountered thus far during the research:

- "(" and ")" for grouping;
- "⬡" for indicating "some type or value";
- subscripts for the cases of sum types;
- "→" for mapping cases;
- "▶" and "•" for discrete cases and grouping respectively.

9 Case Study

Figure 4 refers. The case study chosen was FParsec[7], an open-source library written in F#. This is a type model, not a token model, so only the structural

---

[5] Although numeric subscripts were considered to distinguish between different para-metrically polymorphic elements whenever necessary, this was found to be a more readable alternative.

[6] A case could be made for "extension/specialization", but this was thought to be too specific; in addition, those terms have particular and established OO meanings.

[7] https://www.quanttec.com/fparsec/.

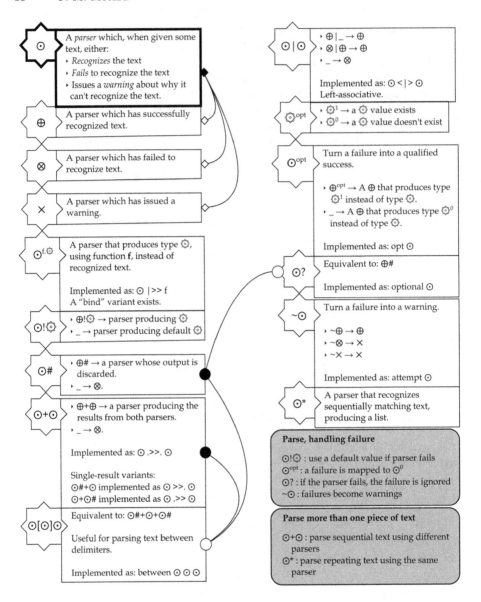

Fig. 4. Case study: FParsec

parts that were considered most important are shown. One consequence of this is that some lesser-documented parts of FParsec, such as its ability to parse expression trees with precedence, do not appear. The model is therefore not a 1-to-1 correspondence with a set of functions and types, but is an abstraction of the problem domain that can be mapped more easily to functional constructs.

The possibility of multiple implementations, all of which follow the same high-level design, is a strength of type modelling as compared to token modelling.

- We begin at the top-left with the definition of a parser, which is followed by symbolic aliases for each of the cases. These ancillary definitions help us greatly later on. The ⊙ definition is foundational for almost all of the other definitions on the page, and is therefore given a thick black border.
- The definition of ⊙$^{f \cdot}$◈ is the first in which we see the ◈, which means "some type or value". The text of definition also indicates that the definition is implemented as an operator in FParsec. The name "f" is repeated in boldface in the definition as a way of showing that it is treated as a substitutable name. All non-alphabetic characters, such as the ".", are considered to be fixed parts of the symbolic definition.
- ⊙!◈ is the first appearance of ▶ and ⌐. The ▶ indicates the start of each new case. In text, one can read the definition as:
  - "If the ⊙ is a parser which has successfully recognized text (i.e. ⊕), then the result is the type that is specified after the '!' mark."
  - "Anything else results in a failed parser (i.e. ⊗)."
  Notice how the ⊕ alias of ⊙ is used to make the mapping simpler to read.
- Skipping ahead, the ⊙[⊙]⊙ parser is the first one in which we see the text "Equivalent to:". Such textual definitions are quite common in functional programming, which is to be expected since functional programming naturally lends itself to composition of functions. The implementation code does not necessarily involve composition, though the "relies" relationships do indicate that core functionality is (plausibly) delegated to ⊙# and ⊙+⊙. "Equivalent to:" should therefore be regarded as referring to semantics.
- ◈^{opt} shows a case where the alphabetic text is not freely substitutable. The textual definition makes it clear that the only two values that are possible are "0" and "1".

In most cases, some attempt is made to express the human-relevant meaning of the operation apart from its formal semantics. For example, the textual definition of ⊙^{opt} begins with "Turn a failure into a qualified success".

The first six definitions thus show most of the features of the "definition" element of the notation. Due to the way in which definitions are ordered, a reader will never have to do more than scan *up* to find the meaning of a definition. At the bottom-right, one can see two etymology sections which should be easy to distinguish visually. Each of these begins with a title describing the group, and a list of definitions follows. It is envisaged that the etymology elements will be most useful for stakeholders who want to understand subtle differences and those who are interested in the different ways to achieve a particular task.

10   Conclusion

This work identified a significant research gap and set out to discover whether the underlying mathematical background of functional programming could be used to inform the high-level structural modelling of a functional system. The answer is an affirmative: the mathematical and functional sides, both grounded in a strong philosophical foundation, lead to a relatively simple diagrammatic notation that should be easy to build upon. Perhaps more importantly, the separation of conceptual semantics from the actual modelling notation, and the grounding within a stable philosophy, should make it possible to build further diagrams or a better notation using the same underlying concepts. Three relationships, inspired by etymology, thesauri and dictionaries, have been proposed.

As stated in the introduction, this work is part of a broader effort to allow functional programs to be modelled in an intuitive way. The modelling itself has been built up as carefully as possible, avoiding the pitfalls of starting with a model that is focused on a particular problem domain or choosing a particular language to be paradigmatic of the functional paradigm. If these precautions were not taken, the history of our field shows that it would be very easy to end up with either a domain-specific modelling language (DSML) or language peculiarities creeping into a modelling notation.

Programming languages are clear to programmers. A Haskell programmer reading the following Haskell code might have a good idea of what it does, even without any further program context:

```
deleteTask p ts = [ t | t <- ts, not (p t) ]
```

However, is it clear to non-programming stakeholders? It can be *made* clear, certainly, but non-programmers have to do the work. Modelling works from the other way around. It can be a shared notation for collaboration by making the otherwise-opaque (but programmer-friendly) parts more accessible. If the proposed notation or a successor achieves this outcome, then it is successful.

In a sense, structural modelling of a functional system is the easier kind of modelling since analogues from mathematical discourse are readily available. It is behavioural modelling and the extraction of a design-relevant rhetoric for functional programming that may be much more difficult. Many questions remain, and much future work remains to be done. Some of the most interesting immediate questions are:

– How "natural" is the notation for non-functional programmers, or for those who are learning functional programming? What changes should be made to evolve the notation?
  • How does one handle symbols and namespacing, so that the same symbols can be used in another context?
  • What is considered to be an overwhelming accumulation of symbols? What do rich, sparse, and poor symbolic vocabularies look like? What design guidelines should exist?
  • What is modelled in a type model depends on what *needs* to be modelled. Which needs are specific to functional programming?
– What might a notation based explicitly on categories, but rooted in the same philosophy, look like? Can previous work in this area [6,14,36] be used to imagine such a notation or improve the proposed notation?

- More of the underlying philosophy and linkages has been summarized than is strictly necessary for a purely structural notation. This is intentional and opens the door to the creation of behavioural models, task- or process-oriented models, and so forth. What might these look like?
- Real dictionaries include parts of speech (e.g. "v.", "adj.", "n.", "informal", etc.) and other annotations which tell the reader about the grammatical and contextual use of the word. Which equivalent notations might the field of functional programmers agree upon? Is it *useful*—and if so, why?—to annotate entries with "mon.", "arr.", "lazy", "async", or "app."?
- It is plausible that the proposed relationships are not the only or most suitable types of relationships to represent. Are there complementary or more suitable relationships that deserve recognition?
- Is a similar notation possible for untyped functional programming? What changes would need to be made?
- How amenable are pure functional programs to model-driven engineering?

Acknowledgments. The author would like to thank the anonymous reviewers of both MODELSWARD'21 and TFP'21 for their constructive and helpful comments on an earlier version of this paper. Insightful and constructive pre-presentation reviewer comments also made this work much better than it would otherwise have been, as did questions and discussions at Lambda Days 2021. This work is based on the research supported partly by the National Research Foundation of South Africa (Grant Number: 116794). This work was undertaken in the Distributed Multimedia CoE at Rhodes University, with financial support from Telkom SA and CORIANT. The author acknowledges that opinions, findings and conclusions or recommendations expressed here are those of the author and that none of the above mentioned sponsors accept liability whatsoever in this regard.

References

1. Armstrong, D.J.: The quarks of object-oriented development. Commun. ACM (2006). https://doi.org/10.1145/1113034.1113040
2. Cardelli, L.: Type Systems. The Computer Science and Engineering Handbook (2004). https://doi.org/10.1145/234313.234418
3. Church, A.: The Calculi of Lambda Conversion (AM-6). Princeton University Press, Princeton (1941). https://doi.org/10.1515/9781400881932
4. Denning, P.J.: The profession of IT: beyond computational thinking. Commun. ACM **52**(6), 28–30 (2009). https://doi.org/10.1145/1516046.1516054
5. Eklund, P., Galán, M.A., Medina, J., Ojeda-Aciego, M., Valverde, A.: A graphical approach to monad compositions. Electr. Notes Theoret. Comput. Sci. (2001). https://doi.org/10.1016/S1571-0661(05)80041-6
6. Fong, B., Spivak, D.I.: An Invitation to Applied Category Theory. Cambridge University Press (2019). https://doi.org/10.1017/9781108668804
7. Ganesalingam, M.: The Language of Mathematics. Springer, Heidelberg (2013). https://doi.org/10.1007/978-3-642-37012-0
8. Ghosh, D.: Functional and Reactive Domain Modeling. Manning Publications Co., Shelter Island (2016)

9. Gibbons, J.: Functional programming for domain-specific languages. In: Zsók, V., Horváth, Z., Csató, L. (eds.) CEFP 2013. LNCS, vol. 8606, pp. 1–28. Springer, Cham (2015). https://doi.org/10.1007/978-3-319-15940-9_1

10. Henderson-Sellers, B., Gonzalez-Perez, C., Eriksson, O., Agerfalk, P.J., Walkerden, G.: Software modelling languages: a wish list. In: 2015 IEEE/ACM 7th International Workshop on Modeling in Software Engineering, pp. 72–77. IEEE (2015). https://doi.org/10.1109/MiSE.2015.20

11. Henderson-Sellers, B.: On the Mathematics of Modelling, Metamodelling, Ontologies and Modelling Languages. Springer, Heidelberg (2012). https://doi.org/10.1007/978-3-642-29825-7

12. Henderson-Sellers, B.: Why philosophize; why not just model? In: Johannesson, P., Lee, M.L., Liddle, S.W., Opdahl, A.L., López, Ó.P. (eds.) ER 2015. LNCS, vol. 9381, pp. 3–17. Springer, Cham (2015). https://doi.org/10.1007/978-3-319-25264-3_1

13. Henrix, J., Plasmeijer, R., Achten, P.: GiN: a graphical language and tool for defining iTask workflows. In: Peña, R., Page, R. (eds.) TFP 2011. LNCS, vol. 7193, pp. 163–178. Springer, Heidelberg (2012). https://doi.org/10.1007/978-3-642-32037-8_11

14. Hinze, R., Marsden, D.: Equational reasoning with lollipops, forks, cups, caps, snakes, and speedometers. J. Log. Algebraic Methods Program. (2016). https://doi.org/10.1016/j.jlamp.2015.12.004

15. Huet, G.: Axiomatisations, proofs, and formal specifications of algorithms: commented case studies in the Coq proof assistant. In: Schwichtenberg, H. (ed.) Logic of Computation. NATO ASI Series, pp. 157–199. Springer, Heidelberg (1997). https://doi.org/10.1007/978-3-642-59048-1_5

16. Jeuring, J., Magalhães, J.P., Heeren, B.: Generic programming for domain reasoners. In: Trends in Functional Programming, vol. 10, pp. 1–16 (2014)

17. Kamp, H., Van Genabith, J., Reyle, U.: Discourse representation theory. In: Gabbay, D., Guenthner, F. (eds.) Handbook of Philosophical Logic, pp. 125–394. Springer, Dordrecht (2011). https://doi.org/10.1007/978-94-007-0485-5_3

18. Kosar, T., Mernik, M., Carver, J.C.: Program comprehension of domain-specific and general-purpose languages: comparison using a family of experiments. Empir. Software Eng. 17(3), 276–304 (2012). https://doi.org/10.1007/s10664-011-9172-x

19. Kühne, T.: Matters of (meta-)modeling. Softw. Syst. Model. 5(4), 369–385 (2006). https://doi.org/10.1007/s10270-006-0017-9

20. Lackey, D.P.: What are the modern classics? The Baruch poll of great philosophy in the twentieth century. Philos. Forum 30(4), 329–346 (1999). https://doi.org/10.1111/0031-806X.00022

21. Li, Q., Chen, Y.-L.: Data flow diagram. In: Modeling and Analysis of Enterprise and Information Systems: From Requirements to Realization, pp. 85–97. Springer, Heidelberg (2009). https://doi.org/10.1007/978-3-540-89556-5_4

22. Lonsdorf, B.: Professor Frisby's Mostly Adequate Guide to Functional Programming (2020)

23. Mac Lane, S.: Categories for the Working Mathematician. Springer, New York (1978). https://doi.org/10.1007/978-1-4757-4721-8

24. Mernik, M., Heering, J., Sloane, A.M.: When and how to develop domain-specific languages. ACM Comput. Surv. 37(4), 316–344 (2005). https://doi.org/10.1145/1118890.1118892

25. Milner, R.: A theory of type polymorphism in programming. J. Comput. Syst. Sci. 17(3), 348–375 (1978). https://doi.org/10.1016/0022-0000(78)90014-4

26. Moody, D.: The "physics" of notations: toward a scientific basis for constructing visual notations in software engineering. IEEE Trans. Softw. Eng. (2009). https://doi.org/10.1109/TSE.2009.67
27. Motara, Y.M.: String diagrams for modelling functional programming. In: 2020 2nd International Multidisciplinary Information Technology and Engineering Conference (IMITEC), pp. 1–7. IEEE, Kimberley (2020). https://doi.org/10.1109/IMITEC50163.2020.9334072
28. Muller, P.-A., Fondement, F., Baudry, B., Combemale, B.: Modeling modeling modeling. Softw. Syst. Model. 11(3), 347–359 (2012). https://doi.org/10.1007/s10270-010-0172-x
29. O'Regan, G. (ed.): Mathematical Approaches to Software Quality, pp. 1–32. Springer, London (2006). https://doi.org/10.1007/1-84628-435-9_1
30. Object Management Group: Business Process Model and Notation (BPMN), Publication Title: Object Management Group specification (2013)
31. Petricek, T.: What we talk about when we talk about monads. The Art, Science, and Engineering of Programming (2018). https://doi.org/10.22152/programming-journal.org/2018/2/12
32. van der Ploeg, A.: Monadic functional reactive programming. In: Proceedings of the 2013 ACM SIGPLAN Symposium on Haskell - Haskell 2013 (2013). https://doi.org/10.1145/2503778.2503783
33. Schulte, C., Magenheim, J., Niere, J., Schäfer, W.: Thinking in objects and their collaboration: introducing object-oriented technology. Comput. Sci. Educ. 13(4), 269–288 (2003). https://doi.org/10.1076/csed.13.4.269.17492
34. Selinger, P.: A survey of graphical languages for monoidal categories. In: Coecke, B. (ed.) New Structures for Physics. Lecture Notes in Physics, vol. 813. Springer, Heidelberg (2011). https://doi.org/10.1007/978-3-642-12821-9_4
35. Simons, A.J.H., Graham, I.: 30 things that go wrong in object modelling with UML 1.3. In: Kilov, H., Rumpe, B., Simmonds, I. (eds.) Behavioral Specifications of Businesses and Systems, pp. 237–257. Springer, Boston (1999) . https://doi.org/10.1007/978-1-4615-5229-1_17
36. Spivak, D.I.: Category Theory for the Sciences. The MIT Press, Cambridge (2014)
37. Stachowiak, H.: Allgemeine Modelltheorie. Springer, Vienna (1973). https://doi.org/10.1007/978-3-7091-8327-4
38. Stutterheim, J.: A Cocktail of Tools: Domain-Specific Languages for Task-Oriented Software Development. Radboud University (2017)
39. da Silva Teixeira, M.D.G.: An Ontology-Based Process for Domain-Specific Visual Language Design. Universidade Federal do Espírito Santo (2017)
40. Wand, Y., Weber, R.: On the ontological expressiveness of information systems analysis and design grammars. Inf. Syst. J. 3(4), 217–237 (1993)
41. Weber, R.: Evaluating and Developing Theories in the Information Systems Discipline. J. Assoc. Inf. Syst. 13(1), 1–30 (2012)
42. Wittgenstein, L.: Tractatus Logico-Philosophicus. Kegan Paul, London (1922)
43. Wittgenstein, L., Anscombe, G.E.M., Hacker, P.M.S., Schulte, J.: Philosophical investigations. Chichester, Wiley-Blackwell (2009)
44. Wlaschin, S.: Domain Modeling Made Functional. The Pragmatic Bookshelf (2018)

Translating Lambda Calculus into C++ Templates

Vít Šefl$^{(\boxtimes)}$

Faculty of Mathematics and Physics, Charles University, Prague, Czech Republic
`sefl@ksvi.mff.cuni.cz`

Abstract. The C++ template system is capable of performing arbitrary compile-time computations, which is typically exploited in generic programming libraries. However, the template language itself is syntactically cumbersome. A variety of tools, ranging from libraries to dedicated compilers, was created to alleviate this issue. One such approach is translating a functional program into a template metaprogram. In this work, we present a new way of translating functional programs based on lambda calculus into template metaprograms. The translation produces metaprograms with clearly defined lazy semantics and supports common functional features such as recursion and algebraic data types. We demonstrate its viability by providing a proof-of-concept implementation.

1 Introduction

In C++, templates facilitate parametric polymorphism. The system itself is based on type abstraction, substitution, and specialization, which can be used to express arbitrary computations. Moreover, since templates are evaluated during compilation, they can be used to compute arbitrary values before the program is run. We refer to such computations as *metaprograms* [11]. In addition to compile-time computations, metaprograms are frequently used in generic programming.

The template system forms a language within a language. This sublanguage does not have a mutable state nor any of the typical control flow statements, allowing us to treat it as a simple, purely functional language. However, since metaprogramming is outside of its intended use case, it usually requires a large amount of boilerplate code and other similar syntactic annoyances. Language features such as the `constexpr` keyword seek to provide an alternative but are currently not powerful enough to fully replace template metaprogramming.

Consequently, a variety of tools was created to simplify writing template metaprograms. The approaches vary from libraries that hide some of the boilerplate code [1,2,9] to external tools that allow the programmer to write the code in a different language and then translate it back into a metaprogram [3,6].

Since the language of templates is functional, some tools [3,10] choose a functional language as the source language for the translation. Functional languages

This work was supported by the Charles University grant SVV-260588.

V. Zsók and J. Hughes (Eds.): TFP 2021, LNCS 12834, pp. 95–115, 2021.
https://doi.org/10.1007/978-3-030-83978-9_5

are often based on lambda calculus, whose core concepts match the template mechanisms very closely. However, while higher-order functions can be expressed in terms of *template-template* parameters, these parameters are not flexible and need to be handled separately from the standard type parameters.

In this work, we detail a new direct way of translating lambda calculus into template metaprograms that avoids these pitfalls and is compatible with any standard compliant compiler. We then provide the translation of various features commonly found in functional languages: local bindings, recursion, pattern matching, and algebraic data types, as well as a novel formal treatment of the semantics of the resulting metaprograms. In particular, we show that these metaprograms have well-defined, non-strict semantics.

In order to demonstrate the viability of this translation method, we also provide a proof-of-concept compiler for a simple functional language based on this work. The language uses Hindley-Milner type system and its syntax is inspired by Haskell.[1]

This work is organized as follows. In the next section, we discuss other approaches to this problem. The third section gives a brief overview of template metaprogramming in C++. The core translation is laid out in the fourth section and the translation of the additional features in the fifth section. The sixth section details the semantics of the resulting metaprograms. The final section provides examples of integration with regular C++ code.

2   Related Work

The most prominent examples of C++ libraries that facilitate metaprogramming are Boost Hana [2] and Boost Metaparse [9]. These libraries aim to provide an easier and more convenient way of writing template metaprograms. Boost Hana provides a general framework for writing metaprograms, while Boost Metaparse functions specifically as a parser generator. However, since these libraries still operate within C++ itself, they cannot be used to eliminate all boilerplate code.

The other approach is the use of external tools. The main advantage is that these tools hide most of the complexities of template metaprogramming from the programmer.

MetaFun [3] is an example of a tool that translates a simple functional language into metaprograms. The translation is straightforward, making use of template-template parameters to express higher-order functions. To our knowledge, this tool is not capable of expressing currying or lambda abstraction.

This approach to metaprogramming is the closest to the approach chosen by this work. A major advantage is that the resulting metaprograms remain legible to C++ programmers and can, if necessary, be adjusted manually. This flexibility is invaluable when the generated metaprograms need to interact with existing metaprograms, which are generally not immediately compatible.

EClean [10] uses a more complicated process of translation. The input language is translated into an intermediate language, which is then interpreted by

---

[1] https://github.com/vituscze/norri.

a template metaprogram. This interpreter is a graph rewriting engine that evaluates expressions similarly to how compiled Haskell code is executed. A similar approach is suggested by Porkoláb [5].

Note that the translation of the source language can also be performed by a metaprogram. As an example, this hybrid approach is used to extend C++ with a self-contained domain specific language [7].

These methods typically sacrifice clarity and transparency of the translated metaprograms in order to improve their efficiency or to reduce the dependency on third party tools. As mentioned previously, this opaqueness might be undesirable in some situations.

3   Template Metaprogramming

C++ templates facilitate parametric polymorphism. However, when combined with other language constructs such as `static const` or `using`, templates become expressive enough to describe arbitrary compile-time computations. A brief overview of this concept is given in this section.

Listing 1 shows a standard use case of templates. The class definition is parameterized over the element type. This template can then be instantiated with a concrete type and used as a regular data type.

```
template <typename T>
class vector {
  T& operator[](size_t index);
};

using int_vector = vector<int>;
```
Listing 1. Parametric polymorphism in C++

The strength of the template system lies in the ability to define compile-time constants that depend on the template parameter. A template can thus be treated as a function, where the input is the template parameter and the output is the defined constant. The result of a metaprogram is obtained by instantiating the template with the desired arguments.

Compile-time constants can be defined with a `using` statement (for type constants) or as `static const` class members (for value constants). There are other ways of defining compile-time constants (such as enumeration labels), but they are interchangeable as far as template metaprogramming is concerned.

Some values can be promoted to the type level, which allows the metaprogram to treat its inputs uniformly as type parameters. Listing 2 shows how to promote `int` constants. The value is accessed by referring to the `static const` member.

```
template <int N>
struct Int { static const int value = N; };

using int_array = std::array<int, Int<5>::value>;
```
Listing 2. Type-level promotion

A template may also be specialized, providing a more specific definition for a subset of template parameters, which can be used by metaprograms to perform case analysis. The template definition is chosen based on how well the arguments fit the specialization, rather than trying the definitions in some predetermined order. Listing 3 combines template specialization and recursion to implement type-level factorial.

```
template <typename T>
struct factorial;

template <>
struct factorial<Int<0>> {
  using type = Int<1>;
};

template <int N>
struct factorial<Int<N>> {
  using type = Int<N * factorial<Int<N - 1>>::type::value>;
};

factorial<Int<3>>::type::value == 6
```

Listing 3. Factorial function

Similarly, variadic templates may be used to represent ordered sequences and template-template parameters to represent higher-order functions. Listing 4 shows an example of such a function. The first parameter represents a template function, which is then applied twice to the second parameter. To treat a qualified name that depends on a template parameter as a type (template), the **typename** (**template**) keyword must be used.

```
template <template <typename> class F, typename X>
struct twice {
  using type = typename F<typename F<X>::type>::type;
};

twice<factorial, Int<3>>::type::value == 720
```

Listing 4. Higher-order function

4   Translating Lambda Calculus

Lambda calculus is a simple functional language. Template metaprogramming and lambda calculus share some core concepts but the correspondence is not perfect. In this section, we show possible ways of representing lambda calculus as template metaprograms and discuss their advantages and disadvantages. We select one representation to be used as the basis of the translation.

A lambda calculus expression can be either a variable, an abstraction, or an application. The basic idea is to use template parameters or type names as variables, template definition as an abstraction, and template instantiation as an application.

Notice that the code in Listing 4 needs to know which parameters represent a function. However, lambda calculus generally makes no distinction between functional and non-functional parameters.

One option is to consider only the simply-typed lambda calculus. In this variation of lambda calculus, each variable has a concrete type and can thus be used to distinguish between functional and non-functional parameters. The functional parameters can then be expressed as template-template parameters of the appropriate nesting and every other parameter as a regular type parameter.

The main downside of this approach is that a single expression needs to be translated into multiple template metaprograms, one for each combination of parameter arities. Another issue is that template-template parameters cannot be used directly with the `using` statement. Instead, the template structure needs to be reconstructed whenever such a parameter is encountered.

The other option is to unify regular and templated types. Every template parameter can then be treated uniformly as a type. Each template can be associated with a simple type by wrapping the template in another class. The identity function defined in Listing 5 shows an example of this unification. Note that this self-application would not be possible with template-template parameters.

Another advantage of this approach is that the resulting translation is type-agnostic, and may be used with both typed and untyped source languages.

```
struct id {
  struct type {
    template <typename T>
    struct apply {
      using type = typename T::type;
    };
  };
};
```

```
id::type::apply<id>::type == id::type
```

Listing 5. Flexible identity function

The inner class `type` provides a layer of indirection, which is necessary to handle self-referential expressions as well as to simplify the translation of additional features. A direct translation of self-referential expressions would lead to an invalid C++ code due to the use of incomplete types.

The downside is that simple types cannot be used as metaprogram arguments. Instead, these types need to be wrapped in another class. Listing 6 shows a wrapping class and its use with the previously defined identity function.

```
template <typename T>
struct wrap { using type = T; };
```

```
id::type::apply<wrap<Int<2>>>::type == Int<2>
```

Listing 6. Argument wrapping

The full translation of lambda expressions is given in Listing 7. The translation of variables and abstractions matches the earlier translation of the identity function. The translation of applications requires the use of inner classes. The names of these classes, S_1 and S_2, must be unique to prevent name collisions. Similarly, since templates do not allow parameter name shadowing, variables must be fresh.

Note that the class S_1 is not strictly necessary and could be removed by changing the name of the inner definition in the translation of the expression E_1. For simplicity, we do not present this optimization here.

$$\text{translate}(x) \stackrel{\text{def}}{=}$$
```
using type = typename x::type;
```

$$\text{translate}(\lambda x.E) \stackrel{\text{def}}{=}$$
```
struct type {
  template <typename x>
  struct apply { translate(E) };
};
```

$$\text{translate}(E_1\,E_2) \stackrel{\text{def}}{=}$$
```
struct S₁ { translate(E₁) };
struct S₂ { translate(E₂) };
using type = typename S₁::type::template apply<S₂>::type;
```

Listing 7. Lambda expression translation

5   Translating Functional Languages

Pure lambda calculus lacks many features of modern functional languages that make programming more convenient and better tractable. In particular, the program cannot be structured into multiple named expressions and data needs to be encoded as functions. In this section, we address this issue by providing a translation of bindings, recursive definitions, and data types.

5.1   Bindings

A binding is used to associate an expression with a name, which can be used to break the program apart into small reusable definitions. Since metaprograms are already associated with a type name, the translation simply wraps the definition inside an appropriately named class. Local bindings, which are used to name subexpressions, use identical translation. The translation is shown in Listing 8.

$$\text{translate}(x = E) \stackrel{\text{def}}{=}$$
```
struct x { translate(E) };
```

Listing 8. Binding translation

5.2   Recursion

While recursion can be accomplished with the use of a fixed-point combinator, recursive bindings are more convenient to work with.

A template may recursively refer to itself, which can be used to directly translate recursive bindings of the form $x = \lambda y.E(x)$. However, recursive bindings of the form $x = x$ or $x = E_1(x)\,E_2(x)$ present a problem. The translation of the recursive occurrences of x requires the definition of x::`type` which is not available at that point.

One option is to restrict the recursion to functions only. The expression in the problematic bindings may then be η-expanded to $\lambda y.x\,y$ or $\lambda y.E_1(x)\,E_2(x)\,y$.

The other option is to translate the recursive bindings in two steps. In the first step, the recursive bindings are replaced with regular bindings by adding fixed-point combinators. Regular bindings are then translated using the techniques described earlier. This process is described in Listing 9.

$$\text{translate}(x = E(x)) \overset{\text{def}}{=} \text{translate}(x = Y\,\lambda r.E(r))$$

Listing 9. Recursive binding translation

The choice of the fixed-point combinator is not important. We have used the Y combinator which is defined as $\lambda f.(\lambda x.f\,(x\,x))(\lambda x.f\,(x\,x))$. It is sufficient to translate the combinator just once and then refer to it from the rest of the code.

The same result can be accomplished with a handwritten, directly recursive combinator, such as the one shown in Listing 10. This particular implementation is optimized to produce as few nested types and template instantiations as possible.

The main advantage of this approach is its flexibility. There is a large variety of fixed-point combinators that can be used to translate more complex recursion schemes, such as mutual recursion. The direct translation cannot be used in this case because C++ does not allow forward declarations of nested classes.

```
struct fix {
  struct type {
    template <typename F>
    struct apply {
      using type = typename
        F::type::template apply<apply<F>>::type;
    };
  };
};
```

Listing 10. Fixed-point combinator

5.3   Simple Data Types

C++ templates can use non-type parameters in their definition. One subset of these non-type parameters are the values of integral and enumeration types. Such values can be promoted to the type level and then used as regular type parameters. For example, if `Int` is the type promoted version of `int`, then an integer constant can be translated as shown in Listing 11. The values of other data types can be translated similarly.

translate(n) $\stackrel{\text{def}}{=}$
```
  using type = Int<n>;
```

Listing 11. Integer translation

However, standard operators cannot be applied to these type-promoted constants. Instead of translating these operators directly, it might be preferable to collect their implementation into a separate header file to reduce the amount of generated code. The header can then be included with the rest of the translated code. As an example, Listing 12 shows an implementation of boolean negation.

```
struct not_ {
  struct type {
    template <typename B>
    struct apply {
      using type = Bool<!B::type::value>;
    };
  };
};
```

Listing 12. Boolean negation

5.4   Complex Data Types

Simple data types use unary templates with a non-type parameter to store one value of integral type. This approach can be extended to more complex data types by using templates with more parameters. For example, any template with two type parameters can be used to represent type-level pairs. However, as with simple data types, the non-trivial task is implementing operations to manipulate the values of such data types.

Instead of focusing on a particular data type, we describe the translation of a class of data types known as algebraic data types. An algebraic data type is a data type formed as a combination of products (tuples) and sums (variants). These data types, therefore, include all records (tuples without any variants) and enumerations (variants without any tuples).

For each data type, we need to specify how its values are represented, constructed (introduced), and deconstructed (eliminated). Let the data type D consist of m variants. Let $D_i(f_1, \ldots, f_{n_i})$ be a value of D, where D_i is the variant and f_1 to f_{n_i} are the fields.

Representation. The values can be represented in two ways. Each variant D_i can be represented as a unique template with n_i type parameters. If the variant has no fields, a non-templated type is used instead.

The other approach is to use one variadic template with one non-type parameter and a variable number of type parameters. The non-type parameter determines the variant and the other type parameters are the fields. Listing 13 shows such a template.

```
template <int Variant, typename... Fields>
struct data { };
```

Listing 13. Algebraic data type representation

These two representations behave identically in normal situations, but differ slightly when misused.

Construction. A value of D is constructed by picking the desired variant D_i and providing a value for each field. The translation is shown in Listing 14. Like before, the names S_j need to be unique.

$$\text{translate}(D_i(E_1, \ldots, E_{n_i})) \overset{\text{def}}{=}$$
$$\forall j \in \{1, \ldots, n_i\}$$
```
        struct Sⱼ { translate(Eⱼ) };
    using type = data<i, ..., typename Sⱼ::type, ...>;
```

Listing 14. Constructor translation

Instead of constructing D_i directly, it might be preferable to use $\lambda x_1 \ldots x_{n_i}.$ $D_i(x_1, \ldots, x_{n_i})$, which can be partially applied and used with higher-order functions.

Deconstruction. The values of D are deconstructed by performing a case analysis. The input of the case analysis is an expression E which represents some value of the data type D. Each case is described by a clause which is a pair consisting of a pattern pat_i and an expression E_i. A pattern can either be a *wildcard pattern* (represented by an underscore) or a *variant pattern* D_j followed by a sequence of distinct variables x_1 to x_{n_j}. The expression E_i may refer to the variables that appear in pat_i.

We require the patterns to be distinct (up to variable renaming) and the case analysis to be complete (if a variant does not have a corresponding variant pattern, a wildcard pattern must be present).

Case analysis proceeds by evaluating E to a value $D_i(f_1, \ldots, f_{n_i})$ for some i. Next, the corresponding clause $pat_j \rightarrow E_j$ is selected and, if applicable, the variables x_1 to x_{n_i} are bound to the values of fields f_1 to f_{n_i}. The result of the case analysis is then the value of the expression E_j.

A wildcard pattern is selected only when no matching variant pattern is found, which guarantees that the selection of a clause is unique thanks to the distinctness and completeness conditions above.

Case analysis can be translated as a template with one type parameter. The definition of this template consists of a template specialization for each of the clauses. The full translation is shown in Listing 15.

$$\text{translate}(\text{case} E \{pat_1 \to E_1, \ldots, pat_p \to E_p\}) \overset{\text{def}}{=}$$

```
template <typename>
struct _case;
```

$\forall i \in \{1, \ldots, p\}$
  $\text{translate}(pat_i \to E_i)$

```
struct S { translate(E) };
using type = typename _case<typename S::type>::type;
```

$$\text{translate}(D_i \, x_1 \, \ldots \, x_{n_i} \to E) \overset{\text{def}}{=}$$

```
template <typename f₁, ..., typename fₙᵢ>
struct _case<data<i, f₁, ..., fₙᵢ>> {
```
$\quad \forall j \in \{1, \ldots, n_i\}$
```
    struct xⱼ { using type = fⱼ; };
  translate(E)
};
```

$$\text{translate}(\_ \to E) \overset{\text{def}}{=}$$

```
template <typename>
struct _case {
  translate(E)
};
```

Listing 15. Deconstructor translation

If a variant contains no fields, the corresponding template specialization is a full specialization. An example of full template specialization is shown in Listing 16.

```
template <>
struct _case<data<0>> { };
```

Listing 16. Full template specialization

Until C++17, a full specialization of a class could only occur at the namespace level. When working with older C++ compilers, only partial specialization should be used, which can be accomplished by adding an extra type parameter to the **data** template. The value of this parameter is irrelevant since it is never used.

As presented, the **_case** template cannot distinguish between two variants of different data types. This is not a problem if the source language can guarantee that case analysis is only performed on the correct values. If no such guarantee exists, it is preferable to represent each variant with a unique template instead of using the generic **data** template.

A more complex case analysis with overlapping cases or nested patterns can be implemented in terms of the simple case analysis given here [4].

As an example, Listing 25 uses this encoding on a singly-linked list.

6   Semantics

In order to show that the translated metaprograms behave in a consistent way, we first only consider strongly normalizing expressions of the source language (expressions whose reduction always terminates). We then show that these metaprograms reduce in normal order. Note that this section only accounts for the relevant portion of the underlying template model [8].

6.1   Preservation

Consider a well-behaved expression in the source language. We need to show that the translation preserves reduction. In particular, we need to consider function application, local bindings, and case analysis. The reduction behavior of operations on promoted data types, once fully applied, is simply given by the underlying C++ computational model. A step-by-step explanation is also available.[2]

Function Application. Reduction of function application is given by the β-rule $(\lambda x.M)N \rightsquigarrow M[x := N]$. The translated metaprogram (Listing 17) unpacks the inner **type** of the lambda abstraction and then instantiates the inner template **apply**, which contains the translation of M. The instantiation replaces all free occurrences of x with the class S_2. Notice that these variables now refer to S_2::**type** which is the translation of N. Thus, the resulting metaprogram matches the translation of $M[x := N]$.

```
translate((λx.M) N) =
   struct S₁ {
      struct type {
         template <typename x>
         struct apply { translate(M) };
      };
   };
   struct S₂ { translate(N) };
   using type = typename S₁::type::template apply<S₂>::type;
```

Listing 17. Reduction of function application

Note that since we require variables to be fresh, the substitution does not have to consider the capture of free variables or variable shadowing.

Local Bindings. The reduction of non-recursive local bindings is given by let $x = N$ in $M \rightsquigarrow M[x := N]$. We can see that the free occurrences of x in the translation of M (Listing 18) directly refer to the translation of N and the resulting metaprogram thus matches the translation of $M[x := N]$.

---

[2] https://github.com/vituscze/norri/blob/master/semantics.md.

translate(let $x = N$ in M) =
```
struct x { translate(N) };
```
translate(M)

Listing 18. Reduction of local bindings

Case Analysis. The reduction of the case analysis (deconstruction) is given by case $(D_i(N_1,\ldots,N_j))\{\ldots,D_i\,x_1\ldots x_j \to M,\ldots\} \rightsquigarrow M[x_1 := N_1,\ldots,x_j := N_j]$. If the constructor tag does not match any of the patterns, the wildcard pattern, which must be present, is used. Without loss of generality, we only consider the case of a unary constructor.

The translated metaprogram (Listing 19) constructs the encoded value of the algebraic data type in the class S. S::`type` contains the constructor tag i and its second parameter refers to the translation of N.

translate(case $(D_i(N))\{\ldots,D_i\,x \to M,\ldots\}$) =
```
template <typename>
struct _case;

template <typename f>
struct _case<data<i, f>> {
  struct x { using type = f; };
  translate(M)
};

struct S {
  struct S₁ { translate(N) };
  using type = data<i, typename S₁::type>;
};

using type = typename _case<typename S::type>::type;
```

Listing 19. Reduction of case analysis

S::`type` is then given to the template class `_case`. Since the constructor tags are unique across the template specializations, the encoded value matches at least one specialization (case analysis is guaranteed to cover all cases) and at most two specializations (one with a matching tag and one wildcard).

In case there is only a single match, C++ has no choice but to use that match. When there are two matches, C++ prefers the more specific match, which is the specialization with the matching constructor tag. In either case, the correct template specialization is selected.

Once the correct specialization is instantiated, the value stored in the encoded constructor is wrapped in the class x and the final result is the translation of M, which can refer to the translation of N via the variable x. This result matches the translation of $M[x := N]$.

6.2   Evaluation Order

Two Phase Compilation. Template code is compiled in two phases. In the first phase, the compiler only processes the parts of the code that do not depend on the template parameters. No instantiation takes place at this time. This phase ensures the template is well-formed, even if it is never used.

The second phase occurs when the template is used with concrete arguments. This forces the instantiation of the template, substituting the template parameters with the given arguments. Code that depends on those parameters can be processed at this time.

In some cases, first phase processing might be undesired. As an example, static_assert which unconditionally fails with a given message can be used to give clearer error messages to partial functions. However, such assertion would be triggered during the first phase processing, before the function is even used.

First phase processing can be avoided by tricking the compiler into assuming the code depends on the parameter. The template always_false in Listing 20 does not depend on the template parameter, but to see that, the compiler needs to instantiate the template. As a result, the static assert in the template succeeds does not see that its parameter is false during the first phase processing and the assert is only triggered when the outer template is instantiated during the second phase processing.

```
template <typename T>
struct always_false
{ static const bool value = false; };

template <typename T>
struct fails {
  static_assert(false);
};

template <typename T>
struct succeeds {
  static_assert(always_false<T>::value);
};
```

Listing 20. Fake parameter dependency

Instantiation. C++ templates distinguish between implicit and explicit instantiation. Implicit instantiation occurs when a code refers to the template in a context that requires its definition. Explicit instantiation occurs as a result of a special instantiation statement.

```
template <typename T>
struct s { using type = int; };

s<int>::type x = 5;        // implicit
template struct s<int>;    // explicit
```

Listing 21. Implicit and explicit instantiation

Explicit instantiation of a class template forces the instantiation of all its members, whereas implicit instantiation only instantiates whatever is necessary. In other words, implicit instantiation is lazy.

Laziness. The translation exploits the previous observation by using the inner type name `type`. The classes are set up in such a way where referring to the class itself does not force instantiation of any of its members. Referring to the inner type name `type` forces their instantiation, which drives the evaluation. Another benefit of this approach is that the translation does not need fake parameter dependencies.

This difference is best exemplified on the encoding of algebraic data types. Notice that the arguments passed to the `data` template are of the form x::`type` for some x. This observation suggests that those data types are strict. And indeed, a C++ compiler will quickly hit the template instantiation limit when trying to compile an infinite data structure.

However, we are not forced to access the inner `type` member when creating an encoded value. We can change the translation of the constructor from Listing 14 and the pattern from Listing 15 as follows.

$$\text{translate}(D_i(E_1, \ldots, E_{n_i})) \overset{\text{def}}{=}$$

```
∀j ∈ {1,...,nᵢ}
   struct  Sⱼ { translate(Eⱼ) };
using type = data<i,  ...,  Sⱼ,  ...>;
```

$$\text{translate}(D_i\, x_1 \ldots x_{n_i} \to E) \overset{\text{def}}{=}$$

```
template <typename x₁, ..., typename xₙᵢ>
struct _case<data<i, x₁, ..., xₙᵢ>> {
   translate(E)
};
```

Listing 22. Non-strict algebraic data types

And indeed, when a metaprogram is translated using this modification, it can create and operate on infinite data structures. Value recursion also functions as expected.

While the translated metaprograms are lazy, it is also possible to force strict evaluation. For example, the `seq` operation from Haskell's `Prelude`, which forces the evaluation of its first argument and then returns the second one, can be implemented by translating $\lambda xy.y$ and replacing the translation of y by the code in Listing 23.

```
template <typename X, typename Y>
using _snd = Y;

using type = _snd<typename x::type , typename y::type >;
```

Listing 23. The seq operation

Notice that when translating top-level bindings, the translated metaprograms are not contained in any template. As a result, they will be evaluated during compilation regardless of whether they are used. If necessary, we can simply wrap these metaprograms inside a template class as shown in Listing 24.

```
template <typename _T>
struct tmp_impl {
    translate(x_1 = E_1; ...; x_n = E_n)
};

using tmp = tmp_impl<void>;
```

Listing 24. Top-level template wrapping

6.3 Compilation Errors

Translated metaprograms produce error messages during compilation if their reduction gets stuck or does not terminate. As a result, well-behaved expressions in the source language translate into metaprograms that do not produce error messages. Thanks to lazy evaluation, this guarantee extends even to expressions that are well-behaved only under a certain evaluation order.

However, C++ compilers impose a limit on the template instantiation depth, which can result in compilation failure even for well-behaved metaprograms. Compilers typically emit a specific error which makes this issue easy to diagnose. If necessary, compiler flags can be used to increase this limit (for example -ftemplate-depth in GCC).

While the translation itself does not avoid compilation errors, most of these errors can be removed by restricting which expressions are valid in the source language. For example, simply-typed lambda calculus is strongly normalizing and its reduction does not get stuck. All expressions are thus well-behaved and if translated, the resulting metaprogram can only fail to compile due to the template instantiation depth limit.

In essence, template compilation errors can be transformed into type errors in the source language. Such errors are much easier to understand and correct.

7 Practical Examples

In this section, we provide two examples of combining the resulting metaprograms with existing metaprogramming code.

The translated metaprograms can often be used directly. Nevertheless, an auxiliary metaprogram can simplify the code, such as when manipulating encoded data types. Instead of a list, we might wish to use a pack of template parameters. This representation is not only more succinct, but it also allows the pack to be expanded into expressions.

Suppose that a strict list data type consists of a nullary variant *Nil* and a binary variant *Cons*, and the encoding uses explicit names instead of the generic **data** template. Listing 25 shows a conversion between such lists and template parameter packs. Note that template parameter packs are not first-class citizens of C++ and must, therefore, be wrapped in an auxiliary template pack. The add metaprogram adds a new element to a template parameter pack. The list encoding is recursively constructed by to_list and deconstructed by from_list.

```cpp
template <typename...>             struct pack;
template <typename, typename>      struct add;
template <typename...>             struct to_list;
template <typename>                struct from_list;

template <typename T, typename... U>
struct add<T, pack<U...>> {
  using type = pack<T, U...>;
};

template <>
struct to_list<> {
  using type = Nil;
};

template <typename T, typename... U>
struct to_list<T, U...> {
  using type = Cons<T, typename to_list<U...>::type>;
};

template <>
struct from_list<Nil> {
  using type = pack<>;
};

template <typename T, typename U>
struct from_list<Cons<T, U>> {
  using type =
    typename add<T, typename from_list<U>::type>::type;
};
```

Listing 25. List conversion

Similarly, existing metaprograms can be adapted for use in higher-order functions. Unary predicates from the type_traits header can be adapted as shown in Listing 26. This process can be automated and extended for predicates and functions of higher arity.

```cpp
template <template <typename> class F>
struct predicate {
  template <typename T>
  struct apply {
    using type = Bool<F<typename T::type>::value>;
  };
};
```

Listing 26. Type function conversion

7.1 Precomputation

Since metaprograms are evaluated during compilation, they can be used to pre-compute constants. The main advantage of this approach is that the computation can be parametrized, which is especially useful when multiple constants depend on a small set of input parameters.

One example is the precomputation of small prime numbers, which is useful when generating large prime numbers. This computation comes with a natural tradeoff: the more time we spend precomputing primes during compilation, the less time we spend finding primes during run time. The metaprogram generates prime numbers smaller than a given value, which gives us control over the tradeoff.

$diff = \lambda step\ start\ list.\ \text{case } list$
  $\{ Nil \rightarrow Nil$
  $,\ Cons\ x\ xs \rightarrow \text{case } compare\ x\ start$
    $\{ LT \rightarrow Cons\ x\ (diff\ step\ start\ xs)$
    $,\ EQ \rightarrow diff\ step\ (start\ +\ step)\ xs$
    $,\ GT \rightarrow diff\ step\ (start\ +\ step)\ (Cons\ x\ xs)$
    $\}$
  $\}$

$sieve = \lambda list.\ \text{case } list$
  $\{ Nil \rightarrow Nil$
  $,\ Cons\ x\ xs \rightarrow Cons\ x\ (sieve\ (diff\ x\ x^2\ xs))$
  $\}$

$between = \lambda x\ y.\ \text{case } x \leq y$
  $\{ False \rightarrow Nil$
  $,\ True \rightarrow Cons\ x\ (between\ (x\ +\ 1)\ y)$
  $\}$

$primes = \lambda n.\ sieve\ (between\ 2\ n)$

Listing 27. Sieve of Eratosthenes

The metaprogram is based on the sieve of Eratosthenes. The generated primes are stored in a list, which is then used to initialize an array. The definitions can be found in Listing 27. The *compare x y* expression answers whether x is less than, equal to, or greater than y.

The list of prime numbers is obtained by applying the *primes* function to the upper bound. The function generates a list of candidate numbers up to the bound and then performs the sieve operation. At each step, the head of the list x is marked as a prime number, and multiples of x (starting with x^2) are removed from the remainder of the list.

Once these definitions are translated into a C++ metaprogram, the resulting list can be accessed as `primes::type::apply<wrap<Int<n>>>::type` (for some number n).

The list cannot be used to directly initialize an array. Instead, the list needs to be converted into a template parameter pack, which can then be expanded into the array initializer. A template parameter pack T, whose elements are types that contain a `value` constant, can be expanded via `{T::value...}`. Listing 28 details how to automate this process.

```cpp
template <typename>
struct to_array;

template <typename... T>
struct to_array<pack<T...>> {
  static const int size = sizeof...(T);
  static const int data[];
};

template <typename... T>
const int to_array<pack<T...>>::data[] = {T::value...};
```

Listing 28. Array initialization using a template parameter pack

And finally, Listing 29 shows how to combine these operations to initialize and use a precomputed array of prime numbers.

```cpp
using list  = primes::type::apply<wrap<Int<50>>>::type;
using array = to_array<to_pack<list>::type>;
for (int i = 0; i < array::size; ++i)
  std::cout << array::data[i] << " ";
```

Listing 29. Precomputed array usage

7.2   Generic Programming

Template metaprograms are commonly employed in generic programming. As an example, metaprograms from the `type_traits` header are frequently used to check the prerequisites of the elements of standard library containers. These operations range from checking whether the element type supports a given operation to manipulating types in an iterator definition.

Suppose we want to create a pool allocator for a set of types. A pool allocator allocates a large chunk of memory at the start, which is then divided evenly into blocks large enough to hold a value of any of the given types. Allocation proceeds by finding an empty block and returning it. Empty blocks can be tracked using a linked list, which allows the operations to function in $\mathcal{O}(1)$ time.

The allocator first ensures that all types meet the given criteria. The *check* function is used for this task. Its input is a list of predicates and a list of types. The check succeeds if all types satisfy all predicates. It is implemented in terms of the *all* function, which checks whether all elements of a list satisfy one predicate.

The block size is also calculated during compilation. The *blockSize* function computes the size of the block as the maximum size among the input types, which is then rounded to the nearest power of two by the *nextPower* function. The expression *max x y* denotes the maximum of x and y. The *size* function computes the size of its input.

The definitions can be found in Listing 30. Two auxiliary functions are used: *foldr* and *loop*. The *foldr* function combines all elements of a list into a single value, using a combining function and an initial value. The *loop* function repeatedly applies a given function to a value while a condition holds.

$$foldr = \lambda f\,z\,list.\,\text{case } list$$
$$\{Nil \rightarrow z$$
$$, Cons\,x\,xs \rightarrow f\,x\,(foldr\,f\,z\,xs)$$
$$\}$$

$$loop = \lambda p\,f\,x.\,\text{case } p\,x$$
$$\{False \rightarrow x$$
$$, True \rightarrow loop\,p\,f\,(f\,x)$$
$$\}$$

$$all = \lambda p.\,foldr\,(\lambda x\,r.\,p\,x\,\wedge\,r)\,True$$
$$check = \lambda ps\,xs.\,all\,(\lambda p.\,all\,p\,xs)\,ps$$
$$nextPower = \lambda n.\,loop\,(\lambda x.\,x\,<\,n)\,(\lambda x.\,2x)\,1$$
$$blockSize = \lambda ts.\,nextPower\,(foldr\,(\lambda x\,r.\,max\,(size\,x)\,r)\,1\,ts)$$

Listing 30. Type check and block size calculation

The *size* function is defined separately as an auxiliary metaprogram in order to use the `sizeof` operator. The definition can be found in Listing 31.

```
struct size {
  struct type {
    template <typename T>
    struct apply {
      using type = Int<sizeof(typename T::type)>;
    };
  };
};
```

Listing 31. Type size metaprogram

Listing 32 shows a possible definition of such an allocator. For the sake of brevity, the allocator only checks one predicate (`std::is_pod`). The predicate list `predicates` and the type list `types` are passed to the translated `check` metaprogram and its result is used in `static_assert`, which halts the compilation and reports the specified error message if the check fails.

Similarly, the type list `types` is passed to the translated `blockSize` metaprogram and its result is used to initialize the `block_size` constant, which can then be used in the appropriate allocation operation.

```
template <typename... T>
struct allocator {
  using predicates = to_list<predicate<std::is_pod>>;
  using types      = to_list<T...>;
  static_assert(check::type::apply<predicates>
                    ::type::apply<types>
                    ::type::value);
  static const int block_size =
    blockSize::type::apply<types>::type::value;
};
```

Listing 32. Allocator for a set of types

8   Conclusion

While recent C++ standards offer more options for performing compile-time computations thanks to the `constexpr` keyword, the support of type-level programming is still lacking. Template metaprogramming thus remains an important tool for implementing generic data structures and functions. However, template metaprograms are often hard to read and write. Some tools seek to alleviate these problems by translating functional code into metaprograms.

We present a new way of translating functional code based on lambda calculus into template metaprograms. The main advantages of our method are its simplicity and well-defined, non-strict semantics. The translation uses direct rules and the resulting metaprograms can be easily incorporated into existing C++ code. The translation can be used with both typed and untyped languages, and also includes bindings, recursion, and complex data structures.

Since the source language is based on an existing programming paradigm, a wealth of existing programming techniques can be reused. Similarly, the source language can be subject to existing optimizing transformations. We hope that this work encourages programmers to write more complex metaprograms as well as to simplify the existing ones.

References

1. Abrahams, D., Gurtovoy, A.: Boost.MPL library (2004). http://www.boost.org/
2. Dionne, L.: Boost.Hana library (2020). http://www.boost.org/
3. Érdi, G.: MetaFun: Compile Haskell-like code to C++ template metaprograms (2011). https://gergo.erdi.hu/projects/metafun/
4. Maranget, L.: Two techniques for compiling lazy pattern matching. Technical report, INRIA (1994)

5. Porkoláb, Z.: Functional programming with C++ template metaprograms. In: Horváth, Z., Plasmeijer, R., Zsók, V. (eds.) CEFP 2009. LNCS, vol. 6299, pp. 306–353. Springer, Heidelberg (2010). https://doi.org/10.1007/978-3-642-17685-2_9

6. Porkoláb, Z., Sinkovics, Á.: Expressing C++ Template Metaprograms as Lambda Expressions, pp. 97–111. Intellect (2009)

7. Porkoláb, Z., Sinkovics, Á., Siroki, I.: DSL in C++ template metaprogram. In: Zsók, V., Horváth, Z., Csató, L. (eds.) CEFP 2013. LNCS, vol. 8606, pp. 76–114. Springer, Cham (2015). https://doi.org/10.1007/978-3-319-15940-9_3

8. Siek, J., Taha, W.: A semantic analysis of C++ templates. In: Thomas, D. (ed.) ECOOP 2006. LNCS, vol. 4067, pp. 304–327. Springer, Heidelberg (2006). https://doi.org/10.1007/11785477_19

9. Sinkovics, A.: Boost.Metaparse library (2020). http://www.boost.org/

10. Sipos, Á., Zsók, V.: EClean - an embedded functional language. Electron. Notes Theoret. Comput. Sci. **238**(2), 47–58 (2009)

11. Veldhuizen, T.: Expression templates. C++ Report **7**, 26–31 (1995)

ProofViz: An Interactive Visual Proof Explorer

Daniel Melcer[1]([⊠])[iD] and Stephen Chang[2][iD]

[1] Northeastern University, Boston, MA 02115, USA
melcer.d@northeastern.edu
[2] University of Massachusetts Boston, Boston, MA 02125, USA
stephen.chang@umb.edu

Abstract. We introduce PROOFVIZ, an extension to the Cur proof assistant that enables interactive visualization and exploration of in-progress proofs. The tool displays a representation of the underlying proof tree, information about each node in the tree, and the partially-completed proof term at each node. Users can interact with the proof by executing tactics, changing the focus, or undoing previous actions. We anticipate that PROOFVIZ will be useful both to students new to tactic-based theorem provers, and to advanced users developing new tactics.

Keywords: Proof assistants · IDEs · GUI tools

1 Introduction

The Curry-Howard correspondence [3,8] is a fundamental insight connecting logic and programming. Specifically, a proposition in a logic corresponds to a type in a programming language, and a proof of that proposition is a program inhabiting that type. In such a language, type checking corresponds to proof checking, and in this manner program properties may be directly verified in the language without resorting to external specification languages or tools. This influential insight has been applied to a wide variety of features such as polymorphism, concurrency, and resource consumption, and has inspired the creation of numerous languages and proof assistants such as Coq, Agda, Idris, LF, NuPRL, F*, HOL4, and Lean (Wadler [18] recently surveyed its history in detail). Collectively, these tools are pushing the boundaries of software development and have even been used to verify parts of some mainstream software [5,19].

These proof assistants still have a steep learning curve, however, and none of the options for beginners are ideal. Some introductory books, such as *The Little Typer* [7], teach theorem proving via straightforward construction of the aforementioned "proofs as programs". While this method is direct and does not hide anything from the learner, it also does not scale well beyond small examples. Other popular texts [14] rely entirely on a separate "tactic" language to generate the proofs, despite the fact that such scripts are often "inscrutable" [15] because they hide much of the proof information from users.

ⓒ Springer Nature Switzerland AG 2021
V. Zsók and J. Hughes (Eds.): TFP 2021, LNCS 12834, pp. 116–135, 2021.
https://doi.org/10.1007/978-3-030-83978-9_6

We present PROOFVIZ, a new kind of graphical IDE for the Cur [1] proof assistant, that bridges the gap between manual proof construction and tactic-based proofs. We believe this tool will be especially beneficial for new users of tactic-based proof assistants because they can more easily see, and thus understand, the parts of an in-progress proof such as the partial proof term, remaining subgoals, and the location of those subgoals in the proof tree. They can also directly perform actions on the proof such as navigating to proof tree nodes, executing or undoing additional tactics, and saving the actions in order to switch back and forth between our tool and a traditional editor. Our tool can be valuable for advanced users as well, e.g., for tasks such as creating and debugging new tactics, where the ability to see the underlying proof term is crucial. Finally, we conjecture that having an extensible GUI will enable many more helpful actions that are not possible in text-based IDEs, such as widescale refactoring of the proof structure, displaying domain-specific proof information, advanced searching of large proofs, and showing available tactics or hints for possible next steps.

The rest of the paper explains the details, and is organized as follows:

- Section 2 introduces relevant background about the Curry-Howard correspondence and tactic scripts;
- Section 3 presents a larger case study that illustrates how PROOFVIZ smooths the transition to tactic-based proof assistants;
- Section 4 shows that PROOFVIZ can be useful to advanced users as well; specifically it shows, via two case studies, how PROOFVIZ can aid the development of new tactics and the maintenance of existing tactics;
- Section 5 discusses Cur, its tactic system, and PROOFVIZ in more technical detail;
- Section 6 compares the tool to related work; and finally,
- Section 7 evaluates PROOFVIZ, discusses future work and concludes.

2   Background: Tactics vs Proof Terms

According to the Curry-Howard correspondence, a logical proposition corresponds to a type P, and the proposition can be proved by constructing a program p with type P. For example, implication corresponds to the function type, universal quantification corresponds to polymorphism, and logical conjunction corresponds to a product type. Thus, a function with type $(\forall \ (P \ Q) \ (\rightarrow \ (And \ P \ Q)$ $(And \ Q \ P))$ in Fig. 1 (top) proves the commutativity of conjunction. Specifically, if P and Q are any two types, i.e., propositions, then a proof of their conjunction is a pair data structure that combines a value of type P (i.e. a proof of P) with a value of type Q. If we have such a pair, then to "prove" the commuted proposition $(And \ Q \ P)$, we simply need to extract the first and second components of the original proof and combine them in the reverse order.

Such manual proof term construction, however, becomes infeasible as proofs get larger. Thus, many proof assistant programmers use a separate "tactic" language that generates the proof. Figure 1 (bot) shows the same proposition along with a tactic script that proves it, where each line of the script generates one

```
; the following program proves the proposition,
; i.e., has type: (∀ (P Q) (→ (And P Q) (And Q P)))
(λ [P : Type] [Q : Type] [pq : (And P Q)]
    (pair (second pq) (first pq)))


; Alternate proof of the same theorem using a tactic script
(define-theorem (∀ (P Q) (→ (And P Q) (And Q P)))
   (intros P Q pq)
   (destruct pq #:as [p q])
   constructor
   (by-apply q)
   (by-apply p))
```

Fig. 1. (top) A program that proves the commutativity of conjunction; (bot) the same program, generated with a tactic script

piece of the proof term in Fig. 1 (top). Specifically, (intros P Q pq) generates the lambda parameters, (destruct pq #:as [p q]) extracts the components of the pair and names them, constructor creates a new pair, and (by-apply q) and (by-apply p) puts the components into the new pair in reverse order.

Such a tactic script is typically developed in an interactive editor that can execute the script step-by-step and show a snapshot of the in-progress proof at each step. Figure 2 shows a few such snapshots for Fig. 1's proof script. Each snapshot has two parts: the *context* above the dotted line shows known assumptions, and the *goal* below the line shows a part of the proposition that is left to prove. The left snapshot, which shows the state immediately after running the destruct tactic, has a context above the line containing propositions P and Q, as well as proofs of those propositions. Below the line, the snapshot shows that we still must prove the consequent of the implication, i.e., the commuted conjunction. The right snapshot, which shows the proof state immediately after running the constructor tactic step, shows (below the line) that we have two subgoals left to prove, the first of which is q (the second, not shown yet, is p), which can be proven easily by applying the facts that we know above the line.

But here we begin to see a problem, which is that the tactic script by itself does not make much sense to a user who later looks at it, because it hides what is happening: the generation of the proof term. Thus, students who rely too much on tactics might not fundamentally understand how theorem provers work. Instead, they might come away thinking that theorem proving is merely the application of ad-hoc "pattern matching" rules (e.g., a popular textbook [14] often gives advice like "where the goal to be proved is exactly the same as some hypothesis in the context or some previously proved lemma ... use the apply tactic"). Such superficial techniques could hinder learning since they may not scale to larger proofs where the patterns are not as obvious.

```
; Proof state after destruct step        ; Proof state after constructor step
P : Type
Q : Type                                 P : Type
p : P                                    Q : Type
q : Q                                    p : P
--------                                 q : Q
(And Q P)                                --------
                                         q            (subgoal 1 of 2)
```

Fig. 2. Intermediate views of the proof state while stepping through the tactic script in Fig. 1: (left) the proof state after running the `destruct` tactic; (right) the proof state after running the `constructor` tactic

Ideally, a novice could use an IDE that more naturally bridges the gap between manual proof construction and tactic scripts. During an undergraduate independent study, the first author was motivated to create and use such a tool, in order to better understand the connection between logic and programs that underpins the majority of modern proof assistants.

3   A Case Study: `add1+=+add1`

This section presents a more complex example that illustrates how PROOFVIZ smooths the learning curve for beginning proof assistant users. Specifically, we show how to prove a basic arithmetic theorem:

```
(∀ (n j) (== (add1 (+ n j)) (+ n (add1 j))))   ; add1+=+add1
```

3.1   Inductive Proofs, Eliminators, and Equality

This seemingly basic theorem requires that students first learn many additional features of the language. First, it uses `Nat`, an inductively defined family. Inductive families [4], as found in languages like Coq, mostly resemble the algebraic datatypes found in functional languages like Haskell or ML. For example, here is the definition of `Nat` from Cur's standard library, which generates the usual data and type constructors (following *The Little Typer*, we use the more descriptive "add1" name for the successor constructor in this example):

```
(define-datatype Nat : Type
  [z : Nat]
  [add1 : (→ Nat Nat)])
```

Inductive families go beyond plain functional datatypes, however, because they allow parameterization over both types and terms, e.g., the type of an *indexed* list parameterizes over both the type of the list element *and* includes an additional `Nat` value that represents the length of the list.

Every inductive family definition also generates an *eliminator* for that type, which generalizes the pattern matching found in functional languages. Following the terminology of Mcbride [11], the eliminator for natural numbers has the form (elim-Nat n P mz ms) where n is the *target* to eliminate, P is the *motive* that computes the return type of the elimination, and the remaining arguments are *methods* corresponding to each case of the data type: the eliminator returns mz when n is zero and calls ms when n is a successor. Method mz must have type (P z), i.e., the motive applied to zero, while ms must have type (∀ [k : Nat] (→ (P k) (P (add1 k)))), which mirrors a proof by induction: for any k, given a proof of (P k), i.e., the induction hypothesis that results from recursively calling the eliminator with k, we must output a term with type (P (add1 k)). For example, here is addition, implemented with elim-Nat:

```
(define +
  (λ [n : Nat] [m : Nat]
    (elim-Nat
       n ; target to eliminate
       (λ (n) Nat) ; motive
       m ; method for zero case
       (λ [n-1 : Nat] [ih : Nat] (add1 ih))))) ; method for successor
```

The first addend n is the target of elimination and, according to the motive, the result is always a Nat. Specifically, when n is zero, the result is m; otherwise, the result is one plus the result of the recursive call (+ n-1 m).

Finally, since propositions are types, inductive families can be used to define new propositions, where the data constructors are proofs of that proposition. One such proposition is the equality type ==, which comes with a constructor (same x) (sometimes called refl or reflexivity) that represents a proof of (== x x). In other words, we can only construct a proof of equality between two things that are equal.

3.2   Matching Tactics with Proof Terms

Figure 3a shows a program proving our add1+=+add1 theorem. It calls elim-Nat with four arguments: a target n, a motive function, and two methods corresponding to the zero and successor cases. When n is zero, the result is (same (add1 j)), which has the equality type we want, i.e., the motive applied to zero:

$$(\forall \ (j) \ (== \ (add1 \ j) \ (add1 \ j))) \quad ; \text{zero case}$$

When n is not zero, the result of the elim-Nat is the result of applying the second method to two arguments: n - 1, and the result of recursively calling the eliminator with n - 1, where the latter exactly corresponds to the inductive hypothesis in a proof by induction. Using this, we must construct a proof of:

```
; successor case
(∀ (j) (== (add1 (+ (add1 n-1) j)) (+ (add1 n-1) (add1 j))))
```

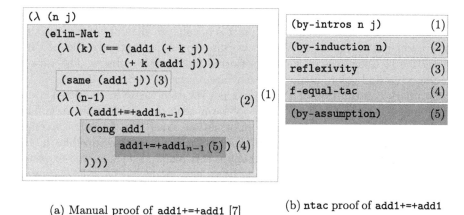

(a) Manual proof of `add1+=+add1` [7]   (b) `ntac` proof of `add1+=+add1`

Fig. 3. The correspondence between a manually constructed proof term and an equivalent tactic script. While these two proofs are written in very different styles, every part of the manual term corresponds to a tactic. PROOFVIZ allows users to view which tactic generated each part of a proof term.

which, when simplified, following the definition of the + function above, becomes:

```
; successor case, simplified
(∀ (j) (== (add1 (add1 (+ n-1 j))) (add1 (+ n-1 (add1 j)))))
```

We can see that this proposition is exactly the inductive hypothesis, with an extra `add1` around it. To go from the inductive hypothesis to what we need, we can use `cong`, which is a theorem about a basic property of functions: $(\forall(A\ B)$ `[x : A] [y : A] [f : (→ A B)]` $(\rightarrow$ `(== x y)` `(== (f x) (f y))))`, i.e., applying the same function to equal values produces equal results.

Figure 3a shows the result of manually constructing a proof term following step-by-step exercises from *The Little Typer*. The same theorem can also be proved via a Cur tactic script, as shown in Fig. 3b. The execution of this sequence constructs a proof term that is remarkably similar to the manually constructed version. A student, however, cannot see this correspondence, nor can they see any of the intermediate proof parts mentioned in this subsection.

3.3 Using PROOFVIZ to Understand Induction Tactics

The two sides of Fig. 3 and their colored components summarize the correspondence between tactics and proof terms that we would like to see. Figure 4 presents PROOFVIZ, which shows this exact correspondence. Briefly, our tool's user interface contains three panes; the tree view, the node information panel, and the interaction panel.

- In the tree view (Fig. 5b), the proof's state is displayed as a tree. A proof tree has a single node that is marked as its "focus", which represents the current proof subgoal. Subsequently executed tactics will add nodes at this focus point, and the tool includes controls to collapse all nodes of the tree that are unrelated to the focus. We are working to further optimize ProofViz's interface to allow concise viewing of other information subsets. The various node types and colors in the tree view are discussed in Sect. 5.2.

– A primary contribution of ProofViz is that each tactic in the proof script is connected to the part of the proof term that this tactic generates. This information is shown in the node information panel (Fig. 5c) when a single node in the tree view is selected. In addition to the list of variables in the context and the types of these variables, this panel also shows the expected output type of the node. Some node types have node-specific information or actions available. For example, "hole" nodes allow for the proof focus to be set to that node (see Sect. 5.2) and "apply" nodes include a list of expected types for its subtrees, as well as the output of the combined result.

– The rightmost interactions panel (also in Fig. 5c) allows the user to execute additional tactics, and the tool allows undoing and redoing an arbitrary number of these interactions. If an error occurs during tactic evaluation, details are printed to the console and the proof tree is not modified.

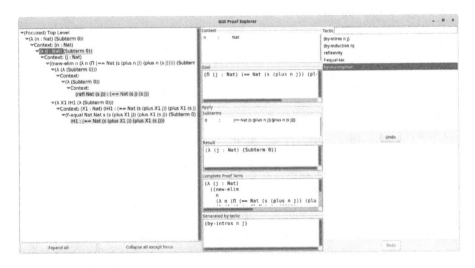

Fig. 4. A view of the interface with a completed proof of add1+=+add1. Note: instead of elim-Nat, Cur uses a general new-elim for inductive datatypes. The cong and same equality constructors are also have different names, f-equal and refl, respectively. ProofViz also shows which tactic generated the selected node, in the middle panel; the user can explore different nodes of the proof without changing the focus.

(a) PROOFVIZ, immediately after running (by-induction n). Information about the currently selected node is visible in the middle panel.

```
▽Top Level
  ▽(λ (n : Nat) (Subterm 0))
    ▽Context: (n : Nat)
      ▽(λ (j : Nat) (Subterm 0))
        ▽Context: (j : Nat)
          ▽((new-elim n (λ n (Π (== Nat (s (plus n j)) (plus n (s j)))))) (Subterm 0) (Subterm 1)))
            ▽(λ (λ (Subterm 0)))
              ▽Context:
                 (Focused) (== Nat (s j) (s j))
            ▽(λ X1 IH7 (λ (Subterm 0)))
              ▽Context: (X1 : Nat) (IH7 : (== Nat (s (plus X1 j)) (plus X1 (s j))))
                 (== Nat (s (s (plus X1 j))) (s (plus X1 (s j))))
```

(b) The tree view after running (by-induction n). There are two holes generated by this tactic; one for the base case, and one for the inductive case. The inductive case has an inductive hypothesis, IH7, available in its context.

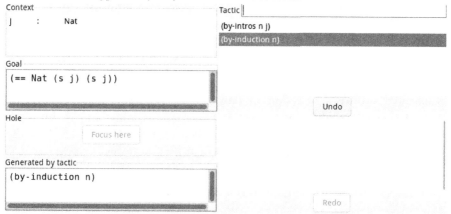

(c) The node information and interactions panel, after running (by-induction n). The selected node shows that it was generated by the induction tactic.

Fig. 5. PROOFVIZ displays all nodes of the proof tree, making it clear to the user how each tactic affects the generated proof term.

Overall, our tool enables users, especially students, to gain more insight into their proofs. For example, with only a conventional view of a proof, the `by-intros` tactic appears to just "move" variables from the goal into the context. With the highlighted correspondences shown in Fig. 3, it becomes clear that `by-intros` really "wraps" the rest of the proof into a lambda. Instead of our goal being a function type (i.e., an implication), we've now assumed a proof of the input type (i.e., the antecedent) and now need only to generate a term with the function's return type (i.e., the consequent). The parameters of the lambda are thus in the context as assumptions when generating the body of the function. Similarly, `by-assumption` merely corresponds to finding an assumption in the context whose type "fits" correctly, and then using its name directly. By exploring the tree view and node information panel in PROOFVIZ, a student can directly see these correspondences and build up their intuition.

Also, our `add1+=+add1` example in Fig. 3 involves inductively defined natural numbers, and thus its proof requires induction. Conventionally, a student might be told to just "use the `by-induction` tactic" as a way to deal with such proofs, but they would not necessarily gain insight into what is actually happening, or why this tactic works. With PROOFVIZ, as seen in Fig. 5a, a student can see what `by-induction` actually does—it creates a `new-elim` node (in Cur `new-elim` is a general eliminator that dispatches to the type-specific ones like `elim-Nat`), and sets up the next subgoals which must be proved. Once those subgoals have proofs, PROOFVIZ shows how they will be assembled into the completed proof term, as highlighted in Fig. 5b.

Lastly, this example gives insight into why tactics are indeed useful, because they can help manage the amount of boilerplate that must be written. For example, with a manually constructed term, the induction motive, a necessary but somewhat formulaic part of an inductive proof, must be written by hand. In contrast, the `by-induction` tactic uses the goal type to automatically generate this part of the term. This type of demonstration conveys the effectiveness of tactics for reducing repetitive code, and may reduce a student's skepticism about whether tactics are even useful.

As seen in this example, we believe that PROOFVIZ can mitigate the steep learning curve associated with proof assistants by showing how each tactic affects the generated proof tree. We envision a student could begin by merely interacting with and exploring a pre-written library of such proofs, while a more advanced student could use PROOFVIZ while writing their own proofs to ensure that the generated proof term matches their intuition of what each tactic does.

4   Tactic Development with PROOFVIZ

Though we have shown how PROOFVIZ can be useful for beginners, it is not limited to only such applications. In this section, we show how PROOFVIZ can help advanced users as well, specifically to develop and debug tactics themselves, where it is often critical to be able to see how the tactics manipulate and generate the underlying proof term.

4.1   Tactic Development: `f-equal`

While PROOFVIZ does not replace traditional testing of new tactics, it can assist with debugging in the course of tactic development. Similar to beginners, tactic developers may find it useful to see exactly how each tactic affects the proof tree. More specifically, in Fig. 3b, we used `f-equal-tac` in our proof script to generate an application of *The Little Typer*'s `cong` theorem but, until recently, the tactic did not exist! We had to add the tactic ourselves and fortunately, we had PROOFVIZ available to help us do this more easily.

Figure 6 summarizes our iterative development process. As a first step, instead of an `f-equal-tac` tactic, we started with an equivalent, but much more complicated, call to a `by-apply` tactic that applies an `f-equal` (Cur's name for the `cong` theorem) function; this is shown in Fig. 6a. Then, we created a new tactic that simply does the same thing as the aforementioned `by-apply`, as seen in Fig. 6b, but this was very verbose and cumbersome to use. We then iteratively improved the tactic so that it could infer all the arguments from the expected goal type, eventually obtaining the simple tactic invocation shown in Fig. 6c. While the implementation details of the tactic itself are not important for this paper, what is important is that after each incremental change, we used PROOFVIZ to verify that the resulting tree structure, subterm types, and generated syntax were what we expected, as shown in Fig. 6d.

4.2   Tactic Maintenance: `by-induction`

When developing PROOFVIZ, we also noticed that the `by-induction` tactic was behaving strangely, but only when used with certain other tactics. Using PROOFVIZ and the information it provides, we were able to quickly discover that the tactic was producing subgoals with incorrect types, as seen in Fig. 7a. Specifically, "Subterm 0" in the figure corresponds to the zero case in our `add1+=+add1` proof from Sect. 3 and thus should have type `(== (s j) (s j))` (Cur uses the name `s` instead of `add1` for the successor `Nat` constructor). Similarly, "Subterm 1" should have a type corresponding to the inductive step in the proof. After deploying a fix for this, PROOFVIZ then allowed us to quickly validate that the revised tactic produces correct goal types, as seen in Fig. 7b. Without being able to see the underlying proof information with PROOFVIZ, debugging and fixing this tactic would have been much more difficult.

5   Implementation Details

PROOFVIZ works with Cur, a new proof assistant [1] that operates in the Racket ecosystem [6], with an emphasis on easy extensibility [2]. This capability has been used to extend Cur with features such as experimental type systems, e.g., sized types, and SMT solver integration. Further, these additional components are modular, meaning that they may be added without changes to any existing languages and do not break existing code, yet they are not isolated like third

```
(by-apply f-equal          (f-equal-tac              f-equal-tac
    #:with Nat Nat s            Nat Nat s
    (s (plus X1 j))             (s (plus X1 j))
    (plus X1 (s j)))            (plus X1 (s j)))
```

(a) An explicit invocation   (b) The first version of   (c) The final invocation of
of f-equal.   f-equal-tac.   f-equal-tac.

```
Goal
 (== Nat (s (s (plus X1 j))) (s (plus X1 (s j))))



Apply
Subterms
 0    :       (== Nat (s (plus X1 j)) (plus X1 (s j)))

Result
 (f-equal Nat Nat s (s (plus X1 j)) (plus X1 (s j)) (Subterm 0))
```

(d) The goal, subterms, and generated syntax for the generated nodes from all three
versions are nearly identical.

Fig. 6. The progression of f-equal forms. Initially, the function needed to be called
manually with by-apply. The first version of the tactic kept all arguments explicit,
but later versions of the tactic inferred all of the arguments from the goal. PROOFVIZ
was used to check that each successive version had the correct behavior. Note that the
name f-equal-tac is used for the tactic to distinguish it from the function.

party tools in other systems. This is because the underlying mechanism—Racket
macros—enables easy communication with other components in the ecosystem.

PROOFVIZ is implemented as a similar extension, and thus its implementation did not require any changes to the core language. It required only minimal
enhancement to ntac, the main tactic system used by Cur programmers, to allow
tagging proof nodes with arbitrary data (discussed further in Sect. 5.2).

5.1   Using PROOFVIZ

Figure 8a shows a basic proof script. A #lang cur on the first line declares the
start of a Cur program. The next require line imports the cur/ntac library,
which contains implementations of many basic tactics commonly used in other
proof assistants. The rest of the program binds id to the term produced by the
subsequent ntac proof script, which proves the identity function type.

To invoke our GUI tool, shown in Fig. 8b, a programmer can simply import
another library, cur/ntac-visual, and then invoke the ntac/visual proof environment. This environment is implemented as an ordinary Racket macro. When
run, the program will launch PROOFVIZ, initially displaying the partial proof

```
Apply
  Subterms
    0   :       (== Nat (s (plus n j)) (plus n (s j)))
    1   :       (== Nat (s (plus n j)) (plus n (s j)))


  Result
    ((new-elim
       n
       (λ n (Π (== Nat (s (plus n j)) (plus n (s j)))))
       (Subterm 0)
       (Subterm 1)))
```

(a) Incorrect intermediate goal types generated by `by-induction`. The term substituted into (`Subterm 0`) must have type (`== Nat (s j) (s j)`); this is the actual goal type of a "hole" node farther down in the subtree.

```
Subterms
  0   :     (== Nat (s j) (s j))
  1   :     (Π (X1 : Nat) (IH1 : (-> (== Nat (s (plus X1 j)) (plus X1 (s j)))) (== Nat (s (s (plus X1 j))) (s (plus X1 (s j))))))
```

(b) The corrected internal goal types for `by-induction`. The "Result" sub-window is unchanged by the fix.

Fig. 7. While developing PROOFVIZ, we found that some tactics produced incorrect goal types at internal boundaries. We were able to use the tool to easily validate the fixes.

generated by the listed tactics (Fig. 4 shows a screenshot). Note that our tool is launched by running the program itself. It is independent of any specific IDE; the proof script itself could have been edited with any editor.

5.2   Implementation

Internally, most tactic systems represent an in-progress proof as a tree. Each tactic then transforms this tree, gradually filling in more information until the proof is complete. There are several varieties of tree nodes in Cur.

A "hole" node represents a node on the tree that must be filled by a value of a specific type. The PROOFVIZ tree view displays this expected type, and highlights the node in red. In an interactive tactic-based theorem prover, hole nodes typically correspond to subgoals. For a proof to be considered complete, the proof tree must not have any hole nodes.

Tactics may also generate "apply" nodes, which combine the values from multiple subtrees into one value of an expected type. For example, an induction tactic applied to the natural numbers will generate an "apply" node with two subtrees. Initially, both of these subtrees will be hole nodes; one with a goal type to prove the theorem for the base case, and one with a goal type for the inductive case. The final piece of an "apply" node is a metafunction to combine the subterms into a larger term that proves the theorem in general. For induction,

```
#lang cur                        #lang cur
(require cur/ntac)               (require cur/ntac
                                         cur/ntac-visual)

(define id                       (define id
  (ntac                            (ntac/visual
    (∀ (A : Type) (a : A) A)        (∀ (A : Type) (a : A) A)
    (intros A a)                     (intros A a)
    assumption))                     assumption))
```

(a) A basic tactic script in Cur   (b) Running our GUI proof explorer

Fig. 8. The addition of PROOFVIZ to an existing proof script. The user must import an extra library, and change the invocation of `ntac` to `ntac/visual`, a macro provided by PROOFVIZ.

this combining function takes as input a proof term that proves the base case and a term that proves the inductive case. Its output is a term that eliminates the inductive datatype value, with the two input subterms placed in their necessary positions. The tree view displays the output of the combining function, even when the apply's subterms contain holes. The implementation of this is further discussed in the **Apply Outputs** subsection below. In the tree view, the places where subterms are substituted into the output of an apply node are highlighted in light gray. An "apply" node can also bind variables that may be referenced in any of its subtrees, by generating a lambda in the output. With induction, for example, inductive cases will include extra variables in their context with the induction hypothesis.

However, an apply node can only provide instructions to the tactic system to assemble pieces of concrete syntax produced by subtrees; these nodes do not provide bookkeeping information about any new names available in the context. "Context" nodes serve this purpose, informing `ntac` that a name is available in a given subtree. These are typically generated as direct descendants of "apply" nodes. The tree view panel shows the names and types of all variables that such context nodes introduce, and highlights such nodes in blue.

An "apply" may also be a leaf node, in which case the combining function takes no arguments and produces a complete term whose type matches the goal. Equivalently, an "exact" node contains a syntax literal to appear in the generated proof term. Exact nodes are highlighted in green.

In summary, apply and exact nodes generate syntax that will become part of the final proof term, while hole and context nodes solely perform bookkeeping functions. There is also a fifth node type for bookkeeping, `ntt-done`, that only appears at the top level of the proof tree. The tree view displays a short summary of each of these nodes' content, allowing the user to see the proof's internal structure at a glance.

Apply Outputs. An "apply" node works by declaring the expected types of a number of subterms. When concrete terms of the correct type are available, the apply node contains a combining function that accepts all of these subterms and outputs a new term; this term is of the apply node's output type. In order to compactly visualize a proof, PROOFVIZ must be able to show the local transformations of each apply node in isolation, without needing to provide a term of the correct type. PROOFVIZ must also show apply nodes in a partially completed proof, where subterms with the expected type may be unavailable.

It is possible to do this because the combining function of an apply node treats each subterm as an opaque value. Thus, to display a string representation of an apply node, the tool creates several placeholder terms that typecheck as the expected type, but show only as (Subterm n), where n is the index of this term in the apply node. These placeholders are used as the input to the combining function when generating the text representation of the apply node. Finally, the output of the combining function is converted into a string and displayed.

Navigation. To allow for the "Focus Here" functionality, the tool generates a sequence of navigation instructions from the top of the proof tree. These instructions are read by a new tactic, navigate, shown in Fig. 9. This tactic starts by setting the focus at the root of the proof tree and then reads the sequence of instructions, which has three possible cases:

– The proof tree's root will always be a marker node, called ntt-done (represented as top-level in the tree view), with a single subtree. Then the path-down-done instruction moves the focus to this subtree. This instruction should only appear in the beginning of the navigate sequence.
– The path-down-context instruction likewise moves the focus to the subtree of the context node.
– The path-down-apply instruction is parameterized with a numeric index. Since an apply node can have multiple subtrees, the index is used to determine which subtree to focus on.

These three navigation instructions are sufficient to jump directly to any location in the proof tree.

```
(navigate (path-down-done) (path-down-apply 0) (path-down-context)
          (path-down-apply 0) (path-down-context) (path-down-apply 1)
          (path-down-apply 0) (path-down-context)))
```

Fig. 9. An example navigation tactic generated by PROOFVIZ. The tactic jumps to the root of the proof tree, then descends to a specific node given by the instructions in the navigation tactic.

Scoping. Since Cur's AST values include binding information that is computed from its context in a program, our tool must be slightly careful about scoping. For example, when `display-focus-tree` is used, since `ntac` has already executed all previous tactics in the proof script outside the context of our tool, if any of these tactics introduced variables into the context, they may not be referenced by tactics executed with the tool.

To work around this, if `ntac/visual` is used, PROOFVIZ executes the proof script as if they were entered in the tool's interactions panel, so all bindings have the proper context. This associates the identifiers with a modified source location, accounting for the reduced source location information that is available when executing the tactic input box's contents.

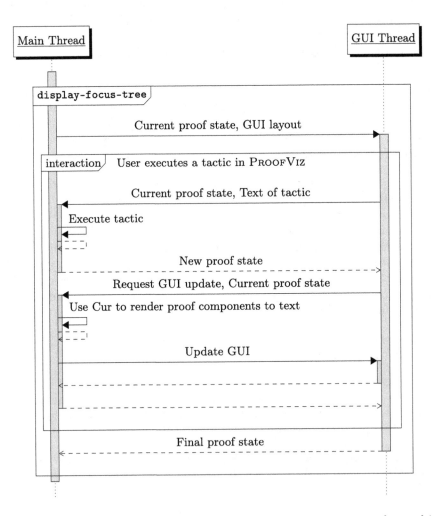

Fig. 10. The threading model for PROOFVIZ, in `display-focus-tree` mode, resulting from constraints on where GUI code and Cur tactics are each allowed to execute.

Threading. Additionally, to further ensure the proper context, PROOFVIZ must be careful when executing tactics in a multi-threaded environment. Specifically, the GUI must run in a second thread because it may start before the main (proof script) program finishes executing. But tactics, to have the same context as the rest of the proof script, must be executed in the main thread. Additionally, during GUI updates, PROOFVIZ must call certain Cur library functions to obtain textual representations of internal tree structures. Due to implementation restrictions, these functions must be run on the main thread as well.

Thus, the tool uses a bidirectional channel to communicate between the main thread and GUI thread. While the GUI is open, the main thread waits on a message from this channel. One such message notifies the main thread that the GUI window has closed, and includes the current state of the proof tree. If `display-focus-tree` was used, the tactic that follows in the proof script receives this proof state as input. The channel also allows the GUI to send arbitrary code to execute on the main thread; this channel ensures that subsequent tactics are evaluated in the correct context. Figure 10 shows the complete threading behavior of PROOFVIZ.

Tree Node Origin Tracking. Most of the features of PROOFVIZ required no changes to any other components of Cur or `ntac`, but the node origin tracking feature required the addition of substructures for each node type. These substructures each add a generic "tag" field, and are interchangeable with the original structures. PROOFVIZ then uses this extra field to associate each node of the proof tree with the node that generated it. However, when `ntac` changes the focus of the tree proof, an implementation detail in `ntac` causes tree nodes to be occasionally deconstructed and reconstructed in the process. The function that does this was modified to detect whether it had destructed a tagged node, and to add the tag back to the new node if it did so. We emphasize that no modifications to Cur's trusted core were necessary to achieve this.

5.3   Unresolved Challenges

Automatically Generated Names. Several tactics automatically generate names for internal variables, often with no way to provide manually-written identifiers. This is typically not an issue, as these names generally would not be exposed to the user. However, when PROOFVIZ encounters one of these identifiers, it can only display the names that have been given to it. To fix this, individual tactics would need to be rewritten to produce meaningful intermediate names. A notable example of this are the names generated by the `by-inversion` tactic, as shown in Fig. 11. In general, we are working to refactor some tactics so they may be more ideally presented in PROOFVIZ.

Ergonomics and Complexity. Relatedly, large proof trees and proof terms can lead to a high information density, or to a GUI which requires excessive scrolling. To combat this, the tree view includes the functionality to collapse

```
Complete Proof Term
((new-elim
  IH
  (λ y60
    IH
    (->
      (== y60 (plus n-1 (s j)))
      (== Nat (s (s (plus n-1 j))) (s (plus n-1 (s j))))))
   (λ eq29
     (new-elim
       (elim-==
        eq29
        (λ y31 _ (match y31 #:return Type ((z) False) ((s X1) True)))
        I)
       (λ _ (== Nat (s (s (plus n-1 j))) (s (plus n-1 (s j)))))))))
 (refl Nat (plus n-1 (s j)))))
```

Fig. 11. A sample proof term generated by `by-inversion`. Here, it is used instead of `by-apply` or `f-equal` in the `add1+=+add1` case study. PROOFVIZ may not be as useful when exploring tactics in which the generated term itself is difficult to interpret.

subtrees which are unrelated to the current focus, and the information about an "apply" node only shows how its direct subterms are used locally. Further work is needed to completely solve the problem, especially as proofs get larger. Fortunately, our presented use cases—assisting beginning students, and creating or debugging new tactics—typically involve smaller, more manageable proofs.

6   Related Work

Visualizing proofs as trees is not new. Even textual proof assistant IDEs, e.g., Proof General, typically support some tree-structured organization of proofs, via the "bullet" system. Proof General also includes some tool-support for graphical visualization [17], which itself is based on a visualization tool in PVS [13]. These proof script visualization tools, however, seem to be exactly that: a visualization of the tactic script that is currently entered in the buffer. While this visualization can help users see the logical organization of a tactic-based proof, this style of visualization doesn't help the user relate the tactic script to the generated proof term, and may be more useful for users who only deal with tactic-based scripts, rather than the users coming from a no-tactics theorem prover. We believe, as illustrated by the previous sections, that an explicit correspondence between the proof term and tactic script is useful for some audiences.

Proof visualizers also exist for non-dependently-typed theorem provers, such as the $\mathcal{L}\Omega\mathcal{UI}$ [16] tool. The SPARKLE [12] theorem prover also provides an IDE-like editing environment for in-progress proofs of a non-dependent functional language. It supports proving properties of many functional features such as laziness, and it interactively shows the context and goals at each point of the proof. It is not based on the Curry-Howard correspondence, however, and thus the proofs generated by its tactics are quite different from the proofs one would construct in a dependently-typed theorem prover based on Curry-Howard.

Several tools visualize the proof tree as a sequent calculus "stack" [9,10], but these tools usually focus solely on the context and goals of each node in the proof tree, rather than the proof term that is generated, and thus don't provide the same intuition to users transitioning from a manual-construction style.

The `Show Proof` command in Coq prints out the partial proof term in the middle of a proof script, but this command lacks the interactivity found in PROOFVIZ. For example, `Show Proof` does not allow the user to view which parts of the proof term are generated by which tactic, and it doesn't display the context and goals of each node in the tree. Furthermore, a call to `Show Proof` must be manually inserted (and removed) at each location where the user is interested in seeing the partial term, while PROOFVIZ enables the user to view and step through all intermediate proof states.

Alectryon [15] aims to allow proof script authors to annotate their proofs and create interactive documentation, enabling readers of this documentation to easily step through the proof state at the current focus. This tool doesn't directly address the generated proof term, which we believe is important for users transitioning to tactic-based proof assistants. However, the tool's motivation highlights many of the same pitfalls of tactic-based programming that can be difficult for such users, thus demonstrating the need for these kinds of tools.

Ultimately, other visualization tools do not aim to address the same issues as PROOFVIZ. Further, they are often tightly coupled with the IDE itself, i.e., the tool must be maintained in sync with the IDE. In contrast, PROOFVIZ is a modular component in the `ntac` tactic system and is independent of how programmers edit their programs. Creating our tool required minimal changes to existing code, and no changes to unrelated tactics. As such, not only is PROOFVIZ itself extensible and well-positioned for future enhancements, it will seamlessly accommodate new tactics, and potentially even changes in the core Cur language.

7   Evaluation, Future Work and Conclusion

The full implementation of PROOFVIZ required approximately 1,000 lines of Racket code. With PROOFVIZ installed, the existing Cur test library of approximately 11,000 lines of code continues to pass. In the course of developing PROOFVIZ, the first author successfully used the tool for dozens of hours, and stepped through thousands of proof script lines. It has greatly enhanced their understanding of dependently typed languages, tactics, and the implementation of theorem provers.

PROOFVIZ continues to be a work in progress. One potential enhancement could be to display available tactics to the user; a related improvement would be the autocompletion of variable bindings or types. A more involved but useful addition could be to illustrate the effect of a given tactic on the proof tree by providing a more direct comparison of the states before and after the tactic is applied. This feature could utilize our existing functionality for relating proof tree nodes to the tactics which generated them. PROOFVIZ could also be modified to automatically save the proof history to a file when closing, instead of printing this to standard output. Finally, extending the undo functionality to full undo/redo-trees would prevent items in the redo buffer from being lost when a tactic is written in the interaction panel. With these and many more enhancements, we hope we will be able to help many more proof assistant users to come.

References

1. Chang, S., Ballantyne, M., Turner, M., Bowman, W.J.: Dependent type systems as macros. In: Proceedings ACM Programming Language 4(POPL), December 2019. https://doi.org/10.1145/3371071
2. Chang, S., Knauth, A., Greenman, B.: Type systems as macros. In: Proceedings of the 44th ACM SIGPLAN Symposium on Principles of Programming Languages. POPL 2017, pp. 694–705. Association for Computing Machinery, New York, NY, USA (2017). https://doi.org/10.1145/3009837.3009886
3. Curry, H.B.: Functionality in combinatory logic. Proc. Nat. Acad. Sci. **20**(11), 584–590 (1934). https://doi.org/10.1073/pnas.20.11.584
4. Dybjer, P.: Inductive families. Formal Aspects Comput. **6**(4), 440–465 (1994)
5. Erbsen, A., Philipoom, J., Gross, J., Sloan, R., Chlipala, A.: Simple high-level code for cryptographic arithmetic - with proofs, without compromises. In: 2019 IEEE Symposium on Security and Privacy (SP), pp. 1202–1219, May 2019. https://doi.org/10.1109/SP.2019.00005
6. Felleisen, M., et al.: The racket manifesto. In: 1st Summit on Advances in Programming Languages (SNAPL 2015), pp. 113–128 (2015)
7. Friedman, D.P., Christiansen, D.T., Bibby, D., Harper, R., McBride, C.: The Little Typer. The Massachusetts Institute of Technology, Cambridge, Massuchesetts (2018)
8. Howard, W.A.: The Formulae-as-Types Notion of Construction. To HB Curry: essays on combinatory logic, lambda calculus and formalism **44**, 479–490 (1980)
9. Kawabata, H., Tanaka, Y., Kimura, M., Hironaka, T.: Traf: a graphical proof tree viewer cooperating with Coq through proof general. In: Ryu, S. (ed.) APLAS 2018. LNCS, vol. 11275, pp. 157–165. Springer, Cham (2018). https://doi.org/10.1007/978-3-030-02768-1_9
10. Libal, T., Riener, M., Rukhaia, M.: Advanced proof viewing in ProofTool. Electron. Proc. Theoretical Comput. Sci. **167**, 35–47 (2014). https://doi.org/10.4204/EPTCS.167.6
11. McBride, C.: Dependently Typed Functional Programs and Their Proofs. Ph.D. thesis, University of Edinburgh (2000)
12. de Mol, M., van Eekelen, M., Plasmeijer, R.: Theorem proving for functional programmers. In: Arts, T., Mohnen, M. (eds.) IFL 2001. LNCS, vol. 2312, pp. 55–71. Springer, Heidelberg (2002). https://doi.org/10.1007/3-540-46028-4_4

13. Owre, S., Rushby, J.M., Shankar, N.: PVS: a prototype verification system. In: Kapur, D. (ed.) CADE 1992. LNCS, vol. 607, pp. 748–752. Springer, Heidelberg (1992). https://doi.org/10.1007/3-540-55602-8_217

14. Pierce, B., et al.: Logical Foundations, Software Foundations, vol. 1, September 2020. https://softwarefoundations.cis.upenn.edu/lf-current/index.html

15. Pit-Claudel, C.: Untangling mechanized proofs. In: Proceedings of the 13th ACM SIGPLAN International Conference on Software Language Engineering. SLE 2020, pp. 155–174. Association for Computing Machinery, New York, NY, USA (2020). https://doi.org/10.1145/3426425.3426940

16. Siekmann, J., et al.: LΩUI: lovely ΩMEGA user interface. Formal Aspects Comput. **11**(3), 326–342 (1999). https://doi.org/10.1007/s001650050053

17. Tews, H.: Prooftree: Proof Tree Visualization for Proof General (2017). http://askra.de/software/prooftree/. Accessed 05 Nov 2020

18. Wadler, P.: Propositions as types. Commun. ACM **58**(12), 75–84 (2015). https://doi.org/10.1145/2699407

19. Zinzindohoué, J.K., Bhargavan, K., Protzenko, J., Beurdouche, B.: Hacl*: a verified modern cryptographic library. In: Conference on Computer and Communications Security (CCS) (2017). https://doi.org/10.1145/3133956.3134043

Author Index

Printed in the United States
by Baker & Taylor Publisher Services